About Mary C. Kocinski

Mary is a self-published author who retrieved a considerable amount of information on the Dorothea Dix Hall Association from her family's summer home attic in New Salem, Massachusetts. She decided to share her discovery by transcribing personal letters from those at the heart of this historical narrative, unwrapping the achievements, power struggles, and selfishness displayed by key people connected with this rare charity.

When she is not writing, Mary enjoys painting portraits, gardening, cooking, or spending time with her family, especially her two little granddaughters. She has four grown daughters and lives with her husband, James, and his cat, Tessa, in New Hampshire.

UNWRAPPING THE PAST
LETTERS FROM THE DOROTHEA DIX HALL ASSOCIATION

by Mary Caroline Kocinski

Copyright © 2018 Mary Caroline Kocinski. All rights reserved.

No part of this book may be reproduced in any written, electronic, recording, or photocopying without written permission from the publisher or author. The exception would be in the case of brief quotations within the critical articles or reviews and pages where permission is specifically granted by the author or publisher.

Disclaimer: although every precaution has been taken to ensure the accuracy of the information contained herein, the author and publisher assume no responsibility for any errors or omissions. No liability is assumed for damages that may result from the use of information contained within.

All primary sources have been transcribed verbatim, with minor edits for clarity. Unless otherwise specified, photos are taken from the author's personal collection.

Published by Adonia James Publishing

ISBN-13: 978-0-692-18700-5
ISBN-10: 0692187006

Cover Design: James Kocinski
Author Photo: Alicia Kocinski
Editor: Ellis Jackson
Writing Coach: Gayle Suzanne

Distributed by Amazon

This book is dedicated to the memory of my mother, Mildred Albert (1923-2017). Her encouragement and enthusiasm were instrumental in my determination to complete it.

Contents

PROLOGUE — ix

PART ONE
1 | BORN OUT OF NEED — 1
2 | KEY MEMBERS, SUMMER TOURS, AND HOTELS — 5
3 | CALM BEFORE THE STORM — 13
4 | HOLIDAYS AND THE LAW — 27

PART TWO
5 | A NEW BEGINNING — 35
6 | ON A MISSION — 49
7 | TUG OF WAR — 61
8 | PLAYING WITH FIRE — 75
9 | A MIXED MAILBAG — 87

PART THREE
10 | HIT OR MISS — 99
11 | ADD AND SUBTRACT — 103
12 | FULL SPEED AHEAD — 107

PART FOUR
13 | CHANGES — 127
14 | FUTURE PLANS — 131
15 | DREAM — 133
16 | THE PLAY — 137
17 | AFTERMATH — 141
18 | THE TRIP — 145
19 | CURTAINS — 147

PHOTO ALBUM — 157
EPILOGUE — 187
BIBLIOGRAPHY — 191

PROLOGUE

Sometimes obscure history can be found in unexpected locations, surviving decades of severe conditions, just waiting to be rediscovered. As a young girl, I discovered the little-known history of the Dorothea Dix Hall Association, a school and home for stage children located in Boston at the turn of the twentieth century. I found boxes and trunks of documents, letters, advertisements, and articles packed away in our summer home attic in New Salem, Massachusetts.

At the time, I was unaware of the scope of my discovery. It was much later, after close examination of the material, that I realized there was a substantial amount of information on the Dorothea Dix Hall left behind by its former owner, Thomas Reddy, a man who undoubtedly was the master behind the scenes. As I transcribed the letters, an interesting story emerged consisting of achievements, disappointments, power struggles, jealousies, and pettiness.

Perhaps there are a few who remember the Hall, the little girls, or their visits to New Salem, but with each passing year the memory fades, leaving the history buried in libraries, old magazines, newspapers, and letters. Assisted by their own words, I offer this unique view to unwrap the history of those devoted to this charity.

PART ONE

THE
Dorothea Dix Hall Association
(Incorporated under the laws of Massachusetts)

748 COLUMBUS AVENUE, BOSTON
TELEPHONE 312-2 ROXBURY

A HOME AND SCHOOL FOR STAGE CHILDREN AND
THE CHILDREN OF ACTORS

1 | BORN OUT OF NEED

Miss Nella Whipple was a self-made, independent woman—a noteworthy accomplishment in the early part of the twentieth century. To some people she was outspoken, headstrong, peevish, childish, and demanding; to others she was a genius. Her dedicated work with stage children was a testament to that, but her skill and energy ended there. She had spread herself too thin, struggling to keep her charitable home and school from closing for lack of support.

At times she expressed her exasperation to the housemaids employed at the Hall. Amanda and Kate listened dutifully as the head matron criticized the changes in her organization. When she reached the threshold of frustration, she sought out Mr. Thomas Reddy and voiced her complaints.

Mr. Reddy, a Boston lawyer, was a patron of children's stage work and had embraced the spirit of Miss Whipple's Dorothea Dix House since its beginning. He persuaded her to incorporate her enterprise to stabilize its fragile existence, thus forming the Dorothea Dix Hall Association. It was affectionately referred to as "the Hall."

However, despite narrowly escaping financial ruin, Miss Whipple did not take kindly to the reduction of her role coupled with disrespect from coworkers. After all, she had co-founded the Hall, and she made it clear in closing one of her letters that her reputation was not to be tarnished.

June 8, 1906

My dear Mr. Reddy,

Oscar Johnson has no shoes. The children have always gone barefooted in the summer, but this year Mrs. Sharp wished them to wear shoes. They wear out on an average of a pair every two weeks and it is very hard to get new ones.

It would be much better to turn down an engagement than to give a poor one and allow the children to lose the reputation they have gained both for good work and good behavior. As far as the concern of the

Dramatic Club, there are so many now trying to run the Dramatic Club that all system has gone. I would rather not have my name used as the teacher for any inferior show that may be given.

Sincerely,
Nella Whipple

Although the children at the Hall were primarily girls, Oscar Johnson was one of the few boys living there. His parents were on the theater circuit and often fell behind on his room and board; this would grate on Miss Whipple's nerves almost as much as his rowdy behavior.

Mr. Reddy's response to the situation arrived in the evening mail.

June 8, 1906

My dear Miss Whipple,

Your letter is at hand. The Johnson boy will get a new pair of shoes, I will see to that. We will discuss the issue with his parents when they return from their tour.

The shoes should not wear out so fast, Miss Whipple. I think it may be prudent on your part not to allow the Johnson boy to scrape his shoes along the sidewalk and cobblestones. I have heard from others that the boy is a rough and tumble child. I myself have witnessed his reckless ways. He needs to learn responsibility, don't you agree Miss Whipple? The fact that our children are well known throughout the community is the reason Mrs. Sharp wants the children to look presentable at all times. We cannot have them running around without shoes. We want to set our children apart from others. These are not ordinary children. We have a lot of work to do to make this organization realize its fullest potential. I am counting on you and seeking your cooperation in all matters, large and small. We have good talented people on board. Let us agree to work together for the good of the Association.

Sincerely,
Thomas F. Reddy

In addition to her caregiving and dramatic work, Miss Whipple spoke on behalf of the Hall's mission through interviews to various publications. One article appeared in *The New England Magazine*. The interviewer, Miss

Margaret Storrs Turner, informed readers about the good work of this rare institution and the financial support it needed to continue operating.

In the article, Miss Turner declared: "Saint Charity has become a lady of fashion. Boston, naturally, is well to the fore in social reforms and institutions, replete with all modern improvement and every advantage of artistic settings. Yet here and there, untouched by the spirit of Back Bay culture, un-patronized by the cream of smart society, hides this or that good work of the modest struggling order, hard to find but worth the visiting, if only for their growing rareness. Such a one, quiet, little known, almost shabby in its entire lack of outward show is the Dorothea Dix Hall, whose little inmates have (so ironical is fortune) lived almost from their cradles amidst the tinsel, glitter and exaggerated emotions, in makeshift splendors of the theater world."[1]

Miss Turner was warmly greeted by Miss Whipple and described her as "a comfortable figure of a woman, dressed with an absolute disregard for fashion, possessing a keen eye, sympathetic smile, and large-hearted capability, which indeed turns out to be her most valuable stock in trade."

The sixteen little actors and actresses were observed as they worked on their assignments. One little girl struggled with her project, using exaggerated facial expressions, as if studying for an upcoming play. The article pointed out that these talented children were the healthiest, prettiest troupe conceivable, and they desired what any home-reared child wanted: love and kindness.

Miss Whipple disclosed, "Some people say there should be no stage children." She was well versed on the subject and had much to say about the dark side of stage business as well as the bright side. She described, with a tinge of regret, how some of her friends had fallen by the wayside because of their live-for-today-the-hell-with-tomorrow attitude, ending up penniless—with unwanted babies, poor health, addictions—or dead. On a positive note, she acknowledged that there were more success stories than not; otherwise, stage business would be fruitless.

The article went on to explain the Hall's early phase and how it grew into an organization for stage children. Miss Whipple, along with two friends, founded a social settlement on Warrington Street. It was intended to assist adult residents, but they soon realized the needs of children were more pressing. The work merged into what was known as The Dorothea Dix Hall, named after the famous philanthropist and Civil War nurse. Miss Whipple took charge as manager of the poverty-stricken charity after her friends left for other endeavors, and the Hall was then exclusively dedicated to educating children of actors and actresses.

---

1. Margaret Storrs Turner, "Dorothea Dix Hall in Boston," *The New England Magazine*, February 1905, 698.

In closing, Miss Turner stated that the staff and workers, most of them volunteers, realized the impact their attention had on these talented, intelligent children, and she agreed that their labors were quite worthwhile.

2 | KEY MEMBERS, SUMMER TOURS, AND HOTELS

Following the incorporation, Mrs. Annie Sharp was appointed general manager, while Mrs. Alice Glover was assigned the role of business manager. Both were independent, talented women whose devotion to their work earned admiration and respect from other charitable groups. Even though they were unpaid workers, they provided countless hours to the charity and assumed responsibilities beyond their assigned positions.

Mrs. Sharp's personal investment was rooted years before the Hall's incorporation, when she was working for Miss Whipple as an assistant. The *Boston Herald* and *Boston Transcript* listed her as hostess for charitable events. Mrs. Glover, also present during the fledgling years, put her business knowledge to use alongside her talents as piano accompanist for concerts. She was outspoken and dedicated.

Both women held a wealth of knowledge about the inner workings of the Hall—the poor condition, the financial struggle, and the lack of sound management. The head matron chose to ignore any advice they offered.

Each spring, Mr. Reddy, Miss Whipple, Mrs. Sharp, and Mrs. Glover secured engagements for the summer tours, an important part of the girls' lives that provided stage education, revenue, and time away from the city. To give other girls a chance to participate, the group was replaced several times throughout the summer. The trips—a combination of rail, carriage, and ferries—were repeated throughout the season, making travel tiresome and uncomfortable; however, the children fared well.

Hotel managers were eager to engage them, as they were an added attraction for guests. Some girls became favorites among the hotel crowd, such as Doris Horslin. Unlike the other children, her parents were not actors. Their daughter was enrolled as a day student and in the dramatics club. She was sent specifically for dance classes to overcome a debilitating condition that affected the use of her legs. She not only recovered but went on to become one of Boston's favorite child actresses, often playing the part of a boy, for boy actors were in short supply. She wowed audiences with her rendition of Little Lord Fauntleroy, a character from the eponymous children's novel by Frances Hodgson Burnett, and the Yama Yama Man, the sinister clown from the operetta *The Three Twins.* Mr. Reddy fondly called her his "best boy."

Alison Black, Stella Craig, Blanche Winters, Juliette Day, Ruth Francis, and Ruth Fielding also ranked among the favorites. Louise Worthington, whose stage name was "Little Winkie," was in high demand on the tours as well as in Boston theaters. She was a winsome little girl, small in stature—a bonus, for it enabled her to portray much younger children.

Favorite resorts and hotels became summer homes for upper-class families. The wife and children remained for long periods, whereas the husband attended to business back in the city, visiting the family on weekends. Because families stayed for most of the summer, the concerts required fresh material since return engagements were frequent and hotel guests had little patience for stale work.

This was the heyday of the grand hotels. Over the years, many were destroyed by fires then rebuilt, only to be burned down again. Those that didn't go up in smoke were torn down, making way for parking lots and condos. Only a few survived that era.

While the girls enjoyed their tour, Mr. Reddy stayed in Boston, juggling Hall duties with his law practice. He ensured that key members were informed on important school matters, such as donations or bequests. His dedication was the glue that kept them together.

July 16, 1906

My dear Mrs. Glover,

I wish to inform you that the Association has received a bequest from the will of the late Mrs. Stevens. Since you are the business manager, I would like you to see the trustee of the will. Dr. Chandler will give you the details. We shall meet with the board and my associate, Mr. Fuller, at a later date to discuss the use of the money.

I would also like a list of your concert schedules. I know it has been difficult, but we do need to continue with our work, even in the light of disappointing receipts. I know that Mr. Fuller has expressed some opposing views on concert work, regardless; I trust you will keep up the good work, my dear Mrs. Glover.

Please keep me posted as to how you and Miss Whipple are getting on.

Sincerely,
Thomas F. Reddy

The business manager acknowledged his letter and apprised him of her frustration with Miss Whipple.

July 18, 1906

My dear Mr. Reddy,

Yours of the 16th received. I will be glad to see the trustee of Mrs. Stevens' will when I hear from Dr. Chandler, which I have not yet. I think myself; there are possibilities in that direction.

Regarding concerts, we went to Marblehead July 11th and to Annisquam July 17th. The only other definite dates are Gloucester, The Moorlands, and the Hawthorn Inn, July 19th and 20th, Colonial Arms, same place, July 23, Magnolia, The Hesperus, July 24, Spring Lake, NJ, August 1st and Peterborough, NH Aug 8th. When we have completed arrangements for Swampscott, Nantasket, and Winthrop I will send you word.

I am beginning to agree with Mr. Fuller that summer concert work does not pay for the loss of time and general wear and tear on eight people. At Marblehead we took $27.09 which about paid for the costumes necessary for the summer work, which is all right, but at Annisquam we only took $12.75 and when you consider that our actual expenses were $8.22 for fares and food, and that it took half of one day, and all night and half of the next day to accomplish this. The gain of about $4.00 is not adequate and I judge from what I have seen already that this will occur more than once. Miss Whipple spent 50 cents for a carriage to leave one poster at the Moorlands Hotel, because if she took a car, she would have to walk about 10 minutes, and this is a fair example of how she spends money foolishly. I find that I will have to be very arbitrary with her, and the concert tour is far from pleasant for me.

I will finish out this summer, according to agreement, but never again with her. We have yet to pay for 100 posters and 5000 programs which will eat up the profits for several more concerts. Unless the Spring Lake trip "pans out" better than I anticipate, I shall advise the board to discontinue the concerts for the remainder of the summer and give the children a rest. If you can't come to any of the Magnolia Concerts, or Gloucester, you will get to come to the nearer places. Come and see me when you can.

Yours sincerely,
Alice L. Glover

A note to Mrs. Glover regarding a board meeting arrived too late; the day before, she and the group boarded a train to Spring Lake, New Jersey. Her annoyance with Miss Whipple had peaked.

August 2, 1906

My dear Mr. Reddy,

I am exceedingly sorry not to be at the board meeting, but we started for Spring Lake NJ yesterday, and arrived here this noon in the pouring rain.

Miss Whipple is making herself very disagreeable on this trip: she told me, in talking things over, that she did not like a stateroom, because it was stuffy, and that she always preferred to take the children in the cabin and have berths. I allowed her to do as she liked, and then, because my husband did not want me travelling that way, got me a stateroom, as he thought it would be better and safer, on account of my having to carry a large sum of money. She was very angry, and hasn't spoken civilly to me for twenty-four hours. She also told me, in the presence of the children, that she declined to be "used as a doormat." I do not understand and am going to ask an explanation when I get her alone. If she persists in this course of action, I shall ask the Board to discontinue the concerts after this trip, which will be a pity, as I am beginning to see results in a financial way. I am sorry not to send you a report for July, but I did not have time to make one out, the evening of the 31st. I had barely opportunity to strike a balance.

Yours sincerely,
Alice L. Glover
Address for 5 days—West Windsor Cottage, Spring Lake, N.J.

The two women grappled over titles and authority. They continued to York Harbor, Maine, and from there Mrs. Glover reported that Miss Whipple seemed better, although she encouraged Mr. Reddy to learn more on the history of the Hall.

August 12, 1906

My dear Mr. Reddy,

Haven't had the time to write before. From Spring Lake we went to Peterborough, NH and from there to York, Maine. And we now expect to return to Boston Aug. 15th although something may occur to change our plans.

Miss Whipple is a trifle better-natured than she was, although I understand that she tells people that I am her assistant. I have not heard her do so, if I should, I might make a few remarks openly. As it is, I think I shall state all of my grievances when I make my report to the board, as she certainly has made things quite disagreeable at times. Financially, I think the concerts are a success, I can tell better a little later.

We are now planning to start for the White Mountains on Monday, August 27th and to fill in the dates between then and the 15th, in and around Boston. Did I tell you that we go to the Atlantic House, Nantasket, on the 20th and that we hope to see you there?

I wish you would go to Mr. Glover's office, room 45 at the Post Office Building, Boston, someday and introduce yourself to him. He can tell you many things which will throw light on The Dorothea Dix Hall affairs. Have you and Mr. Fuller visited the summer and winter houses of D.D. yet? I hope to see you before starting for the mountains.

Yours very sincerely,
Alice L. Glover

Their hostility continued in York Harbor and on a brief stay at the Hall to deliver scheduled area concerts. After fulfilling their obligations, Mrs. Glover prepared her group for the White Mountain trip.

August 16, 1906

My dear Mr. Reddy,

We leave here tomorrow for Boston, and will fill out next week in Nantasket, Marblehead, and other nearby places. We start for the White Mountains Monday, August 27th.

I would like to give up my part of the contract right now, but having promised the Board to see it through, I shall do so. When I report in October, I think Miss Whipple will be surprised. She agreed with me, before we started at all, that there must be harmony between us, and cooperation for the success of the enterprise, also that if either of us had anything to say about not liking things, that it must be said privately and not before the children.

I have carried out my portion of the agreement, but she has acted in a very childish manner, talking to and before the children whenever she was crossed in anything, and out of clear jealousy she has talked to the children about me, and given them orders not to hang around me, not hug and kiss me, because they did not do so with her, and that she has done a great deal more for them than I have or will.

She has also told them that I have no authority on these concerts, that she has it all, and that she would not allow me to play any of the accompaniments, only she is afraid of hurting my feelings. She is planning already what she will do on the concerts next year, but she has not decided whether or not she will take me.

I understand members to say that they wanted me to do the playing, but I could not do it all without having an absolute quarrel with her. She plays four pieces and they are the poorest ones in the show, because she does not know her music, and makes so many mistakes and changes that she puts the children out. I do not pretend to be a star pianist, but I at least play things as they are written.

She has made things very uncomfortable for me all summer, and does not know that I have heard all the things I have; some I have heard her say, and some I have heard the children talking over.

Now, do you not think that my wisest course is to finish out the concert tour without saying a word to her about all this and then spring it all in my report at the Board Meeting in October, and astonish her? I certainly think the Board should know it all, for I cannot do efficient work, while she is so underhanded.

Financially, I think we will come out at least three hundred dollars to the good, although the York trip is not as remunerative as the others.

I am going to tell Mr. Fuller these things I have told you, and then do what you and he and Mr. Glover think wisest.

Do please come to the Atlantic House Concert, at Nantasket, Monday night, August 20, as I want you to hear one of the concerts, without her knowing you are there until it is over.

I will be home Sunday if you want to see me about anything, and if you attend a concert, do not hesitate to speak your mind to both Miss Whipple and myself if you can suggest improvements. I hope you do not mind my grumbling letters.

Yours cordially,
Alice Glover

Mr. Reddy did not make the concert. He encouraged Mrs. Glover to write a letter of complaint and voiced his frustration with the situation.

August 19, 1906

My dear Mrs. Glover,

I will not make it to the Atlantic House to attend the concert. My schedule has been exceedingly full this past week, with both the school and my legal work.

I am so sorry to hear that you and Miss Whipple are still having problems. You can, as you stated, present a letter of complaint to the board for review at the October meeting. I would also like you to define your role in the Association.

The success of this organization depends greatly on the cooperation of the people involved in its day to day workings. I, for one, cannot tolerate any pettiness and unbecoming behavior from the people that have come together to work for a single cause. We, at the Association, appreciate all the hard work and dedication that you have given over the years. I know that your task has not been an easy one, difficult as it is, and made more so by the unwillingness of one who is not eager to contribute or relinquish part of her realm in order to make the Association a success. I have said enough, Mrs. Glover, let the Board decide on how to handle this situation.

Sincerely,
Thomas F. Reddy

3 | CALM BEFORE THE STORM

Mr. Reddy often escaped the demands of the Hall and his practice by spending a few days at his country home in New Salem, Massachusetts. The rural community offered pastoral settings, mountain air, and a slower tempo for the welcomed hiatus. Testimony of his contentment filtered down to his younger brother, Bill, who made the choice to become a permanent resident there.

The house was huge and could accommodate twenty people, at times holding as many as forty guests. The downstairs consisted of a well-stocked kitchen, a long, narrow dining area, a den, and a double parlor that featured a pool table. The second floor housed unique treasures that Mr. Reddy brought back from Egypt and the Middle East. It was in this room that the girls entertained visitors.

A carriage house located at the back of the property stored bicycles and lawn games for the girls. The field across the road included a tennis court, but if the weather was not cooperating, Mr. Reddy and his friends would play a game of cards at the kitchen table. After a pleasant stay, he returned to his law office and the Hall.

Mr. Reddy sought counsel from his longtime friend and confidant, Rev. William van Allen, minister at the Church of the Advent and president of the Hall. The tension between the women had not subsided, and he wanted his friend to be aware of its negative effect on his coworkers and the children. The reverend presented his solution.

Oct 11, 1906

My dear Mr. Reddy,

I am going to N.Y. to give a Retreat Sunday night, not returning until late that week; but, so far as I can now see, I can lunch with you Saturday, if the day suits you. Please send me word tomorrow, or telephone me between half after nine and ten, my office hour.

> *It is certainly important that we straighten things out; and I do not mean to have the good work we have done, in rescuing the work from the unspeakably dirty and poverty-stricken conditions in which we found it, before the incorporation of our association, go to naught.*
>
> *Miss Whipple came to me with her tale of woe; and I told her to put it down in black and white her own ideas of her proper responsibilities and functions for the Board to determine exactly how much of her claim should be allowed.*
>
> *A strict delimitation of frontiers is the best way of keeping peace there; and if she is not willing to abide by the Board's decision, she must abide by the consequences of that refusal.*
>
> *Yours sincerely,*
> *W.H. van Allen*

On October 8, 1906, Mrs. Glover took Mr. Reddy's earlier advice and presented her concerns to the board, though her complaint contained no reference to Miss Whipple by name.

> *To the Board members:*
>
> *The Board of Directors has already listened to the financial report of the Summer Concert Committee, but as the Business Manager, appointed by the Board, I feel that there is yet a word to be spoken in order to make the experience of the past summer of value to the Association and whoever may be selected for next season's manager.*
>
> *The Board will please understand that there are no personalities intended in this report, but justice to everyone concerned demands that it be made, on account of the noticeable lack of co-operation which has prevailed in the summer work, just as it has in the whole past year's work.*
>
> *It is assumed that we are all working for a common object, without thought of self, or desire for any full authority, except such as is absolutely necessary for the proper maintenance of the objects for which the Association was formed, and to this end, the business manager's position should be clearly defined and plainly stated at the time of appointment, and all concerned should be made to recognize it, in order that the dignity of the Association may be maintained, and the misunderstandings, complications and general unpleasantness which has resulted this summer from a mistaken idea of a divided authority, be avoided.*

It is extremely unpleasant for any business manager to be called "an assistant" by one who really holds the latter position and it is decidedly derogatory to the dignity of the corporation to have its so called "mistakes" rehearsed to strangers, when everyone concerned knows that results are what count, and the "mistakes" of this particular corporation have resulted already in the payment of several hundred dollars' worth of debt incurred by the one making the criticism, as well as in a generally improved condition of affairs, including a modest bank account.

Nor was this the only belittling of the dignity of the Corporation, for its business representative was taken to task, that one, for telling the absolute truth in financial affairs, the position being taken that one should always exaggerate such items, for effect, the natural supposition is that a corporation like ours has nothing to conceal or exaggerate in that respect, but if concealment or untruthfulness was desired, then the wrong person was selected for business manager.

With regard to making of engagements for the summer concerts, considerable misunderstanding prevails, The Board of Directors were informed at the beginning of the summer, that no one who had not previously met them could possibly approach the hotel managers, when as a matter of fact, the summer's experience has proven, that given a correct list of the hotels previously visited (which the Board seemed unable at the time to obtain) any member of the Board could have made the engagements, because the children are welcome for the sake of their work, wherever they have appeared.

Engagements have also been secured in hotels which have previously refused to entertain either the idea or the children and these two facts prove, first the efficiency of the training which has been given the children, and second, that task is not wholly confined to one person, and that a neat appearance sometimes adds tact in dealing with strangers.

The question of a neat appearance, on the part of the children, and in fact, everyone connected with the summer concert tour, is one that deserves careful consideration. We cannot expect guest in the best class of hotels to take any special interest in the children or their work unless they and those in charge of them appear well-dressed and presentable at all time.

The wearing of blue denim uniforms has been severely criticized this summer, as savoring too much of the charity school and not comfortable in the hottest weather. There should be two uniforms or suits for each child, one of light and one heavy, and a dainty gown of some description for Sunday wear, as any dress worn a week at a time is too soiled and mussy to make a good appearance, and appearances count for a great deal in the summer concert work. Neat dainty looking children, who are allowed to mingle occasionally and under proper supervision, with other people are much more likely to arouse interest and command attention than a frowsy, unkempt lot who are kept in strict seclusion as if they were objects of which to be ashamed.

This is unjust to the children who should be given all reasonable opportunity to enjoy themselves, in as much as they give their services for the summer's work, and get nothing out of it except a few pennies now and then from the collection and what pleasure they can obtain incidentally.

Justice however has never been strongly marked in dealing with the children connected with the Dorothea Dix Hall in the past, for the policy has always been extremely arbitrary. Apparently the children have never been taught to do right for rights sake, but to avoid direct punishment, which savors too strongly of old-fashioned Calvinism to find favor in the present day. Anyone who knows children at all, know that their sense of justice is strongly developed, much more so in proportion than the average adult's, and any one administering absolute justice is much more likely to command their love, loyalty, and respect than the one who runs the risk of warping their minds and souls by arbitrary fines and sometimes unmerited punishment.

The subject might be continued indefinitely along these lines, but enough has been said to bring to the attention of the Board the matters requiring readjustment and in closing, it is desirable to reiterate and emphasize two points, namely, that the business manager, whoever he or she may be in the future, should be clothed with absolute authority in all matters, and secondly, that this report and recommendations is void of all personal feeling and is made from a sense of duty and responsibility toward the Association, in order that the work in the future may be as far as possible in advance of the past. Progress = Improvement. That should be our watchword.

Respectfully submitted,
Alice L. Glover,
Business Manager for summer of 1906

Two weeks later, Miss Whipple presented her own letter of complaint. The detailed letter gave way to her opinion on her position and ill-advised choices made in the past.

I went one afternoon last summer to see Father van Allen and talk over some things with him. He suggested I write a paper and read it at the first meeting of the board in the fall and that it should be noted and acted upon.

As I have held the Dorothea Dix Hall in my own hands, so to speak, for many years, have had hard knocks, and made many mistakes, have been criticized, both justly and unjustly and learned much by severe experience. It seems to me that it will not be out of keeping for the board to listen to my criticism of their first year's real work that we may all profit by one another's view.

One serious mistake, it seems to me, has been made allowing everything to be decided by one person. This has been made so apparent that Mrs. Glover has been nick-named "The Corporation." I think neither Mrs. Glover herself or the association quite wish such a result. It has been so overdone.

The business, instead of being left with me, as the person naturally next in order to leave it with, has been left with Mrs. Glover's daughter, Dorothy, a child of sixteen years. Thus sometimes when I was in the house, Dorothy transacted the business. This no doubt has been thoughtlessly done but it has been criticized by outsiders as presumptuous.

It seems there has been much complaining but no one has been to me to investigate or ask anything in regard to the complaints made. Apparently all of you are satisfied with one person's view of any matter. This surely is unjust and not quite fair, neither is it wise to listen (as has been done) to the little tattle of children. They are active mischief makers when they find a ready listener and love the excitement and emotion caused by carrying tales—

I wish to speak of the food. The children do the marketing and there are only certain things they are able to buy, hence the food becomes very tiresome—I do not think the children are wise enough to select proper meat. Food is a serious matter, and it does not pay in the end to scrimp that. I do not mean that we must live extravagantly, but, for instance the only fresh fruit the children get is the bit they have in the morning for breakfast—This now is denied them except Sunday's stewed prunes, being substituted, of which one sickens if given too much. The fruit eaten in the morning is a very small expense and necessary to good health. I am told that the children do not pay enough to have fruit. If the children are to be fed according to their pay, they will fare hard. It will indeed be all money and no charity. Groceries have been bought in small quantities, instead of large orders, where in would be a saving of money and bother. I have suggested otherwise but was told that if things were in the house Amanda would use them for supper. Now, we have sent to the treasurer for ten or fifteen cents every night as a rule for something besides bread and tea for the adults. One night, Amanda, instead of getting her fifteen cents, used a can of corn costing ten cents, and so the reprimand.

In regard to the summer—Hough's Neck has not been, it seems to me, much of a success. In the first place it is too near Boston—thus making little change of air. The house is much too small for comfort. So small that the barn had to be used either as a dormitory or dining room and kitchen—sleeping there was out of the question, so it was used for cooking and eating. Built into the corner was an old fashioned toilet, the only one on the premises. This, I told Mrs. Glover when we first looked at the house, should be cleaned at least once a month, but nothing was done all summer and by the end of the season it became almost unbearable and I considered it most unsanitary.

Back in the country, a house could be gotten three times as large for the same amount, perhaps less. At Hough's Neck the children have not been outside the yard. There being no walks or desirable places to go. In the country, where we have been previously, there were all sorts of rambles, wood land walks, picnics, and berrying. The children had all the berries and apples they wanted for the asking—good milk and fresh vegetables at nominal prices. This summer they have scarcely tasted a berry, and strawberries, they did not even smell, while milk was poor and expensive.

If a child was ill or tired, sleep was out of the question as every room was a sleeping room for three or four and no one could rest quietly alone. This has been especially hard on Amanda and Kate who were obliged to sleep in a room with seven others, where every movement could be heard and scarcely an hour passed through the night that one or another child did not arouse, not for aid or to disturb others, but adults awaken easily where children sleep. Amanda and Kate work hard and should have their rest, else it tells on their nerves and carries to the children.

As to going there after the theatre every night—I or anyone else could never stand it, especially as there is no rest after six in the morning. It is rumored that the house is to be hired again next summer. I hope not, for the neighbors are likely to complain. They looked with surprise and have voiced their dislike to so many children huddled together in such small quarters. This feeling has not been helped by the case of scarlet fever there.

The children's clothing has never been as neglected as this summer, they have never looked so ill kept. I speak of this because that is one of the things I was criticized for and that I expected to see bettered. This was perhaps due to the fact that the board wished Mrs. Glover to go on the concert tour but now that you have investigated my work there, perhaps it will be different. Anyone else would assist me just as well on the concert tour, then leaving Mrs. Glover to attend properly to the house children. It was a mistake to send the two heads away. It left things at home no better than here-to-fore—

As to the concerts: This year for the first time in my experience there has been friction. Mrs. Glover claiming to be the head. I naturally disregarded her as head. The business manager does not stand ahead of the manager. Of course I was everywhere the acknowledged head, and Mrs. Glover the assistant. I knew it would be so when we started out, it was of no use for me to talk. I do not see how anyone could expect it to be different. It is not likely that people who have known me as at the head of such work for fourteen years will accept anyone green in the business as superior or is it at all likely that I will ever go out with the children in any other capacity than the head one. Until I do, find someone that is really superior or at least as good or I become incapable—

The business was done just the same as I did it—no better—sometimes not as wise. I had thought myself no kind of a business woman but I begin to think perhaps I have as much business in me as the average woman—I have had years of experience and it has taught me many things. I am fully capable of attending to all the business and everything connected with the theaters and the concerts and with the responsibility of the other work off my hands ought to do well.

Please remember that much of what seemed in years gone by as lax, the impossibility of one pair of hands doing everything properly. There was marketing, sewing, theaters, concerts, children, and letters, everything to do and only myself, and what help I could get from Amanda and Doris, the latter too young to take any fixed stand.

Sometimes, before the advent of Amanda, I have had even the cooking and washing to do in order to make both ends meet. This I did all one summer with the children and three boarders and gave several concerts besides, so you see my path has been far from a bed of roses; but it has been buoyed up by love for the children and knowledge of the necessity of the work.

I am willing to be assistant and take a back seat as far as household affairs go, but the theatrical side—no—I have worked hard for that to give it up, and as yet no one understands it and all its varied workings as I do. That is my sphere. I know it and all others acknowledge it.

The concerts this year have been as successful as here-to-fore. I have personally overseen that they might be. The expenses are less, as we used the old uniforms of last year and got half rate tickets. I myself applied for the tickets some time ago and got them through the kindness of the Children's Aid Society.

I tried in vain to get new capes for the uniforms as they were very shabby—but Mrs. Glover did not seem to wish to get them, so next year everything will have to be new.

I was appointed on a committee of three to arrange the concert affairs but if they have been talked over and plans made, I did not know it. No one has asked my views as regard to any matter, nor have I been notified of any conference.

One cannot serve two masters. There must be one acknowledged head to each department, this has caused all the friction this past year, and this higglety pigglety management is most detrimental to the house, this constant butting in to each other's work. The end of this should come at once, else it will reflect on the character of the children, they quickly learn, to manage both, and are disloyal to each.

My particular forte is the teaching and management of the theatrical and dramatic part of the work, this surely no one could question, and this I wish to look after as my part, interfering with nothing else, but willing to help in the other departments when needed and I can.

Mrs. Glover, or whoever holds the position of matron should look after the house interest and have general supervision of all household affairs, also willing to help me in my department, if she can, when needed. I assure you all, that to have each our own departments is the only way the affairs can be managed properly.

Now much is neglected because of the shifting responsibility, for instance, there is house cleaning, which has not yet been done, blankets to wash, and beds to clean, else there'll be trouble, etc. etc. All these things cannot be left to Amanda, she has her hands full now—anyway—one has to look after such things personally, or else they would never be done right.

Now a suggestion as to the care of the children. I have thought it a good plan to divide the care of their clothes between the four adults of the house—this would give us each five children to look after personally, to be responsible for their appearance. I think the children would be much better cared for in this way.

I know this communication is lengthy but it seemed the only way I could do in order that we all might know of and profit by past mistakes. The successes are not hidden. If we look upon the work of the association fairly and broad mindedly, attend to our separate departments as best we can and look to the conference of the board when things get beyond us or we fear our own judgment, then better work will be accomplished, better results gained.

I have had letters, calls and warnings, many of them—telling me that the Association wished to push me one side. These I have laughed at until this summer when the truth of it was forced upon me by a certain member of the board.

I know that one holding a public position is generally abused and misjudged, more or less, but why, after I have given the best years of my life to this work, have made it a success that it is, unaided—have given it to you after the real burden has been born, why you should wish to trample me out completely with no apparent reason is beyond my comprehension. It is dire ingratitude to say the least, and perhaps I have too much spirit left in me to accept so much without resentment—I have accepted many things dutifully, but in giving you the work, I have not sold you myself, nor can I submit to being treated as a servant or ordered about like a lackey. True, I am a paid worker now, so are some others, Mrs. Glover's rent and heat and house for her family is quite equivalent to a salary.

I realize in every way the advantage of having the house under an association and am gratified to think my work has proved sufficiently important for that. I am willing to make self-sacrifice to a great extent, I have sacrificed everything so far, but I, as the Mother head, so to speak, feel that I am entitled to respect, at least, and I tell you all that my senses, my mind, my brain is still with me. If I happen to be asleep externally, I am far from that internally. I fear if I had been in such a dormant state there would have been no Dorothea Dix Hall for anyone to fight over leadership for.

I hope the board will consider this paper and that you will give me the full control of the dramatic and concert work and all it involves. This is all I ask and I will try to make it successful. I will start the Club anew, which was a dismal failure last year, and devote myself to this work, keeping the concerts up to their high standard.

I asked you to play with me. I now ask you to play fair—
Nella Whipple

She made several valid points about lack of proper diet, the unsanitary condition of the cottage, and the turmoil of too many bosses. Her complaints paled as she asserted her real desire to maintain her position as dramatic instructor. Mr. Reddy sent an outline of what was expected of her in this role.

November 3, 1906

My dear Miss Whipple,

Now that the Dramatic and Concert Committee is appointed, don't you think we ought to get together and do something? If we don't make a big success of this part of our work we are likely to be laughed at and I don't want that. The power is entirely in our hands and it is up to us to make a success or failure.

In your letter of complaint, you made special reference to the failure of the Dramatic Clubs last year and you wish that they might be revived this year and kept up to an excellent standard. I personally join with you in this wish and will give all the time I can to help form these clubs and make them successful, but I fully appreciate that the final success or failure will depend largely on yourself. As I am neither lazy nor neglectful, you can be sure of my hearty cooperation and that of the entire Dramatic Committee.

Among the things we want to carry out are:

1—a house concert at least once a month
2—the preparation of the benefit concert; for the little Winters girl.
3—the preparation of a junior and Senior Dramatic Club and the arrangement for their weekly meetings and the carrying on of the work connections of the same.
4—adoption of means to increase number of concerts

I am going to write to Mrs. Glover & ask her to send me a list of engagements for the Concert Company as fast as made & perhaps the Dramatic Committee can find some way of increasing this part of one's work. I understand there are 2 this coming week at Hyde Park on Wednesday & Thursday evenings I will try & attend one of them. I believe 2 of our boys are at the Bowdoin Sq. this coming week. I would strongly recommend that you look out for the theaters rather than Mrs. Glover and as she will probably go with the concerts any way as I assume there was many. I would recommend that you ask for the charge of these 2 concerts especially as they are "short" ones so that you can give the time to the theaters, otherwise you will have to provide someone to go to the theaters which I think you are better able to handle yourself than anyone else.

Now Miss Whipple, in regard to increasing the business of the concerts, I had in mind recommending to the Concert Committee getting up a printed circular advertising the Association and urging clubs and churches to help the good work along by engaging the Concert Company. These circulars should be sent to all the clubs and churches in this, say 30 miles of Boston, at least & possibly it might pay to advertise in the newspapers.

I will also recommend to the Committee that you prepare as many children as possible for the concert work, picking out from time to time from the house children as well as the Dramatic Clubs those children who show that they process superior talent or ability to advance them as rapidly as possible in this line of work. In this way we can have a large number of children at one time who will be able to do all the work of the present Concert Company & we might be able to use them for engagements when the "first" company is engaged. In this way we are giving a larger number of children an opportunity to appear & prove their ability besides helping them and the association in a financial way.

I have in mind also that this may in the future lead to results of a broader scope than we have yet undertaken but which I think we should go into slowly but surely.

For instance, I had in mind that if we had a large number of children say 50, all of whom processed an unusual amount of dramatic or concert ability, we might be able to produce a show on a scale larger than we have yet undertaken.

I believe however that in an undertaking of this kind we should adopt the methods usually employed by the most successful business men, namely start as we are really now doing, in a small way & gradually increase the work, profiting as we go along by our experiences and correcting our errors. In this way, it seems to me, that we can scarcely fail to be successful.

By following out an ambitious yet conservative policy I am sure we will have the confidence of our friends and if we can attain the ends we contend for we will be amply rewarded by the satisfaction of accomplishing what some think we are likely to make a failure of. We have therefore some little reputation at stake and therefore something to fight for.

(So far as the Committee is concerned, leaving myself out of it, I could not ask for a better one. My colleagues are both very capable and I am sure will be pleasant to work with. Mrs. Sharp has a good business head and does not hesitate to express herself. Mrs. Wade has good original ideas and can give us the benefit of her stage experience when necessary).

With two hardworking, conscientious people like this on a committee I can hardly conceive of failure. Both these ladies in the work they did at the benefit last year set a pace that it will be hard for me to follow out. I will do my best to keep up with them.

This is as much as I want to say now but when the Committee gets together for its first meeting we will probably want you there and we can all then express our views and we shall expect some good ideas from yourself.

With all our ambitious projects in view we shall expect to see you grow thin this winter, but in order that you may not be overworked I think it would be well for you to start Mrs. Glover off on the "short" concert at least so that she will not get mixed up in the theaters and this will give you more time for our work.

Of course in what I say in this letter I am speaking only for myself, but I feel sure the other members, when I can consult them, will approve of it.

I will be glad to have you look over the Columbus Ave house with me this week and will be glad also to have Mrs. Sharp & Mrs. Wade join us if I can get word to them.

Yours truly,
T.F. Reddy

Miss Whipple's role as dramatic instructor had been clarified. The dramatic committee consisted in part of Mr. Reddy, Mrs. Sharp, and Mrs. Glover. Her reaffirmed position did not diminish her mistrust of her coworkers.

Mr. Reddy presented a more in-depth memo to the department heads to clarify roles and duties.

In order to prevent any misunderstanding as to the scope of the powers and duties of the General Manager and the Dramatic Instructor as provided in the By-laws articles two and three, this board hereby declares that the General Manager must not in any way interfere with the duties of the Dramatic Instructor and the Dramatic Instructor must not interfere in any way with the duties of the General Manager and this board hereby declares that it is the intention of the said By-Laws that the General Managers' duties shall relate mainly to the business management and the care of the house and the children and the Dramatic Instructors to the instruction of the child in Dramatic Art and Concert work as well as to carry out such other work as the Dramatic and concert Committee may suggest or provide.

Where the Dramatic and Concert Committee grant privileges to the Dramatic Clubs and Classes and providing a place in the house for meeting and practice the General Manager may make reasonable rules to prevent the abuse of the house privileges and if these rules are violated she shall call the attention of the Committee shall investigate and correct each abuses if they are found to exist.

The Dramatic Instructor shall have the care and discipline of the children while she is instructing them and while they are performing at theaters and concerts and shall be responsible for their travel while at such places while going back and forth. At all other times they shall be under the care & discipline of the General Manager and at such times the Manager shall be responsible for their conduct.

The Housekeeper and her assistant shall be under the charge of the General Manager who shall see that their duties are properly performed. No one is permitted to pay any one for accompanying children to and from theaters it being assumed that there will always be plenty of volunteers for that service.

Miss Whipple is to continue as before to assist the school teachers in the school. The appointment of the house committee with Mrs. Sharp, Mrs. Fuller and Miss Foster will remain in force.

The Dramatic and Concert Committee may permit the use of the concert room in the house for the benefit of any deserving child or children connected with the house and may permit their use by the dramatic Clubs subject [any] reasonable regulation as it may impose.

4 | HOLIDAYS AND THE LAW

The holidays were celebrated in grand style. It was a time when the theatrical community came together and assisted in providing a memorable event for the Dorothea Dix children. Thanksgiving featured a traditional dinner consisting of several turkeys, with all the trimmings and desserts. The Hall overflowed with children, parents, actors, supporters, and patrons. The guests were entertained by the children and later by area actors.

The Thanksgiving celebrations were barely over when plans for the Christmas party were underway. The celebration was aided by donations of money, food, and gifts. The affair, always a news item, was described at length in the *Boston Herald* and *Boston Tribune*.

One supporter, Winthrop Ames, a well-known theatrical producer and theater manager, took a keen interest in the upcoming celebration and offered his help.

December 3, 1906

My dear Miss Whipple,

It's a long time since I have had so much fun as yesterday in watching the children's pleasure; and I want to do something similar for their Christmas pleasure, if you'll let me. Can you tell me now on what-say the Christmas dinner or tree or on whatever they have-comes, that I may make arrangements in advance? Since the entertainers are likely to be busy about that time. Can you also suggest what sort of thing would please them best—is it something in the line of a "show" such as trained dogs, or birds, etc. etc. or something for the Christmas tree or their dinner?

I'm sorry to trouble you about this matter, which is such a selfish pleasure for me, but I want to be sure to be able to do something for your tots if you'll let me.

Sincerely yours,
Winthrop Ames

The support was appreciated. Mr. Reddy donated $30.00 for the event, as described in Mrs. Glover's note.

Dec. 23, 1906

Dear Mr. Reddy,

Yours of the 21st inst. received, containing check for $30.00. Thank you very much for helping out on the tree, as well as for the turkeys, and the hall for the party.
    Don't forget tomorrow night at the Universalist Church, in North Cambridge (take No. Camb[ridge] car to Davenport St.) I agree with you about individual presents to the children. Hoping to see you tomorrow night, I am.

Yours cordially,
Alice L. Glover

The annual Children's Christmas Party was a huge success. Among the guests were representatives of the various theaters of the city as well as others interested in dramatic affairs. Even Santa Claus appeared with his helpers to hand out presents. Each Christmas was a fun-filled day for the children, highlighted by tree trimming, gift giving, and more attention than usual. They spent the evening singing, dancing, and playing until it was time to retire to their rooms.

Once the children had gone, Mr. Reddy unveiled to the adults that a new location for the Hall had been acquired, one that accommodated the growing demands of their work. It was a noisy, happy time; life was good within the warmth of the Hall.

The public mood did not share their contentment. Lawmakers, and the nation, were embroiled in the issue of child labor, compelled by the lectures of Eldridge Gerry, founder of the Society for the Prevention of Cruelty to Children (S.P.C.C.). Mr. Gerry's mission became a fanatical crusade to keep child performers off the stage while adopting a diminished attitude toward the abuse suffered by real child laborers.

There is no doubt that abuse existed within the stage industry. Closer inspection revealed two categories relating to the law: Child Labor and Child Stage Laws. The latter labor laws focused on mill children, factory workers, and children working in dangerous environments; the lesser-known stage laws centered on the safety and well-being of children involved in circus acts, namely acts that included acrobatics or dangerous stunts. "Legitimate" stage children were placed under the umbrella of circus performers. Most offenses were found in the circus, a place where runaways, orphans, and homeless children sought refuge. In some cases, children were sold to—and, in worse cases, kidnapped by—the circus. The frequent beatings and forced dangerous acts were recounted in numerous memoirs of former child circus performers. As for the legitimate stage children, their abuse usually showed up in the form of indulgence and pampering.

Boston, a city that embraced art and culture, had turned away from the obvious abuse of factory and mill children and on to unjust scrutiny of stage children. In the weeks leading up to the party, Rev. van Allen was aware of existing unrest and Mr. Gerry's highly publicized campaign. He wanted to know more about the implications of the law, as it stood, and how it affected the Dorothea Dix Hall.

December 20, 1906

My dear Mr. Reddy,

One of the newspapers published an article about child labour the other day making reference to the fact that some of our Dorothea Dix children were only five and six. I do not know just what is the Massachusetts law concerning stage performances by children; but it is plain that we must be strictly obedient to it. I wish therefore, that you would be so good as to look it up and make an abstract of it for the information of the Board of Directors.

    With very cordial regard, and with all the greetings of the season, believe me, my dear Mr. Reddy,

Yours faithfully,
W.H. van Allen

The information that Mr. Reddy uncovered was complex. The following is a portion of his findings.

No penalty was provided for a violation of these Statutes until 1906, when the Statute provided a maximum fine of $300, six months imprisonment or both, and for a continuance of the employment after notice, a fine of not less than $20.00 per day nor more than $100, or by imprisonment of not more than 6 months. The person liable under this Statute of 1906 was the one who employs, procures, controls or permits a minor to be employed. One who continues to employ was liable for additional penalty.

The Statute in regard to stage children (children under 15 years old) seems to have had for its object, at least partly, the prevention of any abuse or injury to the children physically. This is apparent from the things which are expressly prohibited, such as dancing and acrobatic acts, though perhaps it would be hard to imagine how singing or playing on musical instruments would be any more injurious physically than speaking lines or "running", but however this may be, it does not appear that the Legislature had in mind any purpose to restrain the child from "working" and the matter of whether the child received "wages" or not did not seem to enter into the legislation, the apparent intention being to protect either the physical or moral welfare of the children or both.

Gradually, as we have seen, the laws in regard to child labor became more and more severe, while the Statutes in regard to children on the stage became more liberal.

But suppose such a child appeared in different plays occasionally only, either as a part of his education or to keep up his stage training and experience, as is done by the children of the Dorothea Dix Hall Association of Boston, which as a part of its work, educates such children for the stage and permits them to carry on their stage work, then a different question arises. If such a child's services are volunteered, without compensation, it would seem at least to dispel any suspicion of an employment at work, unless it was done for the purpose of evading the Statutes.

It seems to me, that under these circumstances, a child is not employed at work within the meaning of the Statute.

If a child received compensation for its work, it might affect the matter to this extent. If the child is continuously performing for wages, it would indicate that compensation, and not education was the main inducement, and therefore, it was work. If the child appeared only occasionally and received compensation on those occasional appearances, I think it might be held that this compensation did not alter the fact that the education and experience were the main inducements and therefore, it was not work.

It seems to me that where the child receives compensation, it becomes a question of fact whether the child is employed at work or not, and this would be influenced to a great extent by the frequency and extent of his appearances and the amount of his compensation.

There are excellent reasons too, for taking this view of the matter. A comparison of the Statutes will point out what these are.

In the child labor laws, the word "employment" is constantly used. It is used in the original act and all the way through in all the amendments down to the Statute of 1906 providing a penalty.

In the latter Statute, the penalty is provided for whoever 'employs' and for those who procure or permit the child 'to be employed' and again for those 'who continue to employ,' showing to my mind that the relation of the employer and employee must exist.

The phraseology in the stage act is broader. It says that no person shall 'employ or exhibit or sell, apprentice or give away for the purpose of employing or exhibiting a child etc.

This indicates that the Legislature, in the one case, had in mind only to prohibit the actual employment of children, and in the other, to go farther, and prohibit not merely the employment but the exhibition of children. That the latter might include children who appeared as part of their education was apparent from the exception in the Statute, and that it was the intention to prohibit not merely children who were hired, but who were exhibited was also made clear by the addition of the word 'exhibition.' It is interesting to notice the three expressions used in connection with the things that are accepted.

1—the education of children in music and dancing.
2—their employment as musicians, etc.
3—their taking part in any festivals etc.

The broadest possible language is used in connection with the latter privilege. As stated above, it does not expressly prohibit children appearing in speaking parts or walking or running on and off too.

The full document detailed changes in fines, ages, and types of acts covered under the law for each year of the previous decade. All 32 pages were sent to Rev. van Allen, including remarks and opinions. The reverend stressed adherence to the current law, albeit with the hope that it could later be modified.

Dec. 24, 1906

My dear Mr. Reddy,

Thank you for your very full answer to my question. I have what some people might call a superstitious reverence for law, and have always taken the ground that to disregard law which is still in force, is to lay the foundation of anarchy.

It is perfectly plain that the law in question has lapsed into disuse; but that does not change our duty, and I cannot rest content in a mere passive attitude. Would it not be possible for us to move in this coming legislature, for such a modification of the law as shall give discretionary power to some magistrate to license the appearance of children under proper conditions? It would appeal to the general sentiment of the legislature as well as to the public. How does the proposition strike you?

With heartiest Christmas greetings and with very cordial personal regard, believe me, my dear Mr. Reddy—

Yours faithfully,
W.H. van Allen

PART TWO

5 | A NEW BEGINNING

Miss Whipple's work was a source of great pride. Although she remained suspicious of her coworkers, she rehearsed the girls with the zeal she had when she was solely in charge, honing her craft and introducing new routines. When a song or dance failed to meet her standards, she would ding a small bell that hung from her belt.

The winter concerts were filling up with first-time requests for entertainment.

Jan. 2, 1907

Dear Miss Whipple,

As I am on the entertainment committee for our church fair to be held the first week in February, I thought I'd write to you and ask what your price is for an hours' entertainment.

The only time the children have been in North Weymouth was a year ago at the Fair held in the Pilgrim Church. I was there and enjoyed it immensely and think it would take at our church fair, only first, I must see what it would cost as we are not allowed to spend only about so much. Of course we wouldn't want the same things that were given before, but I presume you keep a record so as not to gin the same thing twice in one village. Please answer as soon as possible.

Mrs. Joshua Holbrook

Letters of inquiry were given to Mr. Reddy to determine the cost. After the price was settled, a date was chosen, girls were selected, and a program was planned. This process took weeks or more to complete.

Jan 9, 1907

Dear Mr. Reddy,

Your letter at hand and after consulting the rest of the committee, I would say that we'd like to have you furnish just the best entertainment you can for us with four children. We figure that will cost us in the neighborhood of $16.00 car fares and all, so I think the price will suit all, right?

Am I not correct? Considering the price settled, about the date. We have our Fair the 6th and 7th of February. Have you a preference as to which night you had rather come. We have home talent the other night so we have no preference. Please state which night-and any other arrangements which are necessary.

If Miss Whipple is the one to come with them and if she wishes to arrange any matters with me personally, I might be able to see her, if I knew where to find her, sometime when I'm in town.

Now there is one other thing which I must speak about, though it may sound peculiar to you. I accidentally heard tonight that the congregational church people who have their fair the week previous to ours, mentioned at their meeting today getting the Dorothea Dix children to entertain one night of their fair. Now at a financial standpoint it is wholly out of the question to think of running similar entertainments for both fairs. So if they consult you about it and you decide to furnish them with an entertainment I should be obliged to gin it up.

This may seem a funny arrangement to you, but this is a comparatively poor town and we depend on some of the people from other churches to patronize us and vice versa. Consequently, the same people wouldn't care to pay out their money to see the same sort of entertainment two weeks running.

Now I don't presume to expect you to do anything different than to consult your own interest in the matter. But I shall be very much disappointed not to have you, and if you decide in their favor-should they ask you, I hope you will notify me immediately as I should have to hustle to get something else.

Hoping to hear from you soon,
Mrs. Joshua Holbrook

A few weeks later, Mrs. Holbrook wrote back to inquire about an opening. There was a miscommunication with a committee member over the program date.

Jan 25, 1907

Dear Mr. Reddy,

Have you still got the 6th of Feb. open or has someone engaged the children for that night? The other member of our Fair committee has a nephew who is a reader and she was going to use him for the other night of the Fair. She wrote and asked him and he replied "either night". So I wrote you that you could set which night you wished. The 7th was chosen and yesterday I was informed by the other member of the committee that the reader couldn't come the 6th. That's what one gets for working one's relatives.

I told her that I'd write you and see if you still had the 6th an open night and if you had not we'd have to let the nephew go and hire someone else's nephew. If you can change the night, well and good, and if not, it's the same. I'm sorry to bother you with another letter but I couldn't do anything different.

Cordially yours,
Mrs. Joshua Holbrook

After a period of relative peace, the tension between Mrs. Glover and Miss Whipple returned.

Jan 28, 1907

My dear Mr. Reddy,

I forgot to remind you last night, that there are two concerts, next week, at Hyde Park, on the 7th and 8th (Thursday and Friday evenings.) Wouldn't it be well for you to tell Miss Whipple that I am to go on the concerts just the same as I have been doing? Also these are what we call half concerts, where we give only half the usual program and use only three children each night. (They are for a church fair.).

Now Miss Whipple will have two boys at the Bowdoin Square Theatre, in speaking parts, besides the children in Peter Pan, and as she herself has said more than once, that only one adult is necessary to conduct a concert with 3 children, she needn't go if you think she ought to be at the theatre. This is the way we used to do it last winter until she got jealous of my good luck in running the concerts alone. She used to go to the theatre, and I used to go to the concert. Of course you will do what you think best, I only tell you this for your information as chairman of the Concert Committee.

Edna has gone home and I sent Theodore with Winkie. I don't know that I should have let Edna come anyway, as she was sliding down the banister when she fell last night, and should be punished by depriving her of some pleasure. I let the children walk, as they wanted to do so, and I am going to give them the money you left for car fare, to have for themselves.

Yours sincerely,
Alice L. Glover

As promised, Mr. Reddy offered the association his interest in a building on Columbus Avenue. It was a three-story brick house containing 17 rooms—five on the first floor, six on the second and third floors—with a water heater and bathroom located on each level. The spacious concrete basement provided an excellent space for rehearsals.

Mr. Reddy's forte was his ability to multitask. He procured new concert dates, worked out legal details for the new residence, and supervised the move. Once the preparations were completed, he and Rev. van Allen focused on the guest list for the house warming. The list included various politicians, clergymen, theater managers, and performers.

January 5, 1907

My dear Mr. Reddy,

I have just written to the Governor, as you suggested, asking him to name a date between the first and the fifteenth of March when he could come to our house warming. As soon as I hear from him, I will let you know. I think that the whole scheme is an excellent one, and have no doubt that it can be made a brilliant success. Our festivity of the other day certainly was that. The more friends we can make in such a fashion, the better for the institution.

But, we must be keeping our eyes open to avert such a complication that arose in New York in connection with our little friends of "Peter Pan."

We must get a committee of ladies at work on the question of furnishings; it ought to be possible to secure gifts of rugs and pictures and such things, laid aside, as not quite good enough for home use, enough to make the house very attractive.

Have you had any talk with Dr. Chandler about the matter of diet? That is one of the most important matters we have to confront?

I hope that you reassured Miss Shaw about Miss Whipple, and I am glad to know that she is improving. With very cordial regard, believe me, dear Mr. Reddy,

*Always yours faithfully,
W.H. van Allen*

The problems cited with the use of children in *Peter Pan* signified the law needed to be clarified. The outcry from certain groups, such as the S.P.C.C., viewed child entertainment as harmful employment. The Dorothea Dix girls occasionally appeared in New York City with Maude Adams in *Peter Pan*, a fact that caused uneasiness among the board members. They wanted to focus on the mission, not on unfavorable attention.

It was vital that the governor and other lawmakers understood that the Hall protected and educated their children against the abuse found in other sectors. Due to increased concern about stage laws, Mr. Reddy presented a bill to the Massachusetts legislature on behalf of the Hall and other similar organizations.

His bill generated support from friends in politics and the theater. One friend was Mary Shaw, a well-known and controversial actress. She was the second vice president of Dorothea Dix Hall and served on the board for many years. Her interest went beyond stage children; she was a feminist and suffragist. In 1907, she starred in George Bernard Shaw's *Mrs. Warren's Profession*, a scandalous play about dishonesty, hypocrisy, and an unrepentant prostitute. An earlier performance in New York City was met with harsh criticism and protests, even involving police raids in some theaters. The play was successfully revived in 1907, due in part to Miss Shaw's candid discussion on the subject matter outside of the performance.

When the rumored conflict between the Hall's women reached her, she wanted answers.

January 31, 1907

Dear Mr. Reddy,

Your statement as to the equity in the property on Columbus Ave offered to the Dorothea Dix Hall Association and the description of the same, received. As far as I can judge it seems an admirable opportunity to secure a house for the organization. I am sorry I cannot be present to deliberate the question with the Board but I have entire faith in the judgment of its members. It will be, as you say, an objective to work for and will place the Association in a more settled position as a philanthropic enterprise.

I have heard a rumor that Miss Whipple is no longer with you. Is this true? And if so, how did it come about? I was the instrument of calling the attention of The Actors Church Alliance to her work, which was then a spontaneous thing, being not incorporated.

I am not in Boston and cannot keep myself in touch as much as I wish but I have heard some disquieting rumors. I expect to be there in February and shall then be able to learn about the work and plans. With all good wishes to you and the house.

Sincerely,
Mary Shaw

Miss Shaw was reassured that Miss Whipple was still at the Hall, albeit unhappy and frustrated.

February 3, 1907

My dear Miss Shaw,

I pray this letter finds you in good spirits. I have read about your revival of "Mrs. Warren's Profession" and hope that this time the reception is warm. You, as always, my dear Miss Shaw, will rise above the controversy.

Miss Whipple is still with us, although she makes it very clear to all who will listen to her that she is not happy with the changes. I fear that her discontent has made it difficult for others to work with her. It also has a negative effect on the children. They are sensitive to any unpleasantness between Miss Whipple and Mrs. Glover. As much as I wanted her to embrace the changes and stay on, I feel that it's a matter of time before she will take her leave.

She owes you a great deal of gratitude for your interest in her work and the introduction to the Actors' Church Alliance. We all owe you a great deal of gratitude, Miss Shaw. Your interest and your continued membership on the board is fully appreciated.

With sincere best wishes, I remain,
Thomas F. Reddy
(The board has approved the new house, all goes well.)

To bring attention to the bill, Mr. Reddy wrote to several influential groups, asking for support of the amendment. He sent a message to Mr. E.D. Price, department manager of promotions at the Actors Fund of America in New York City, an organization that was formed in 1882 and is still in business today. He offered the organization a performance by the children in their upcoming fair.

January 14, 1907

My dear Mr. Price,

I have heard that you are planning an Actor's Fund fair for the benefit of retired stage people. I would be more than delighted to offer assistance in the way of a show given by the children of the Dorothea Dix Hall Association.
As you may have heard, we are involved in adding an amendment to the existing Child Labor laws to allow our children more freedom when it comes to appearing on the stage. You may be aware of our organizations mission, and that is, to promote the best care, welfare, education and opportunity for our children. Their work on the stage is vital to their future employment. Their experience and training has been well regarded by many of the theater managers throughout Boston and the East Coast. I will be seeking support from as many organizations involved with stage people when this bill is presented to the house. I hope to count on you as one of our many supporter[s].
I wish you success in your endeavor, and hope that we may be of assistance to you. I look forward to your response.

Sincerely,
Thomas F. Reddy

Mr. Price responded to the offer and reminded Mr. Reddy that he had, at times, employed some of the Hall's children.

January 16, 1907

My dear sir,

I have read with great interest your letter concerning the Dorothea Dix Hall Association and appreciate your desire to contribute to the success of the Actors' Fund Fair. The latter will not be held until the week of May 6th.

It is too early to determine the exact scope and character of the entertainments in connection with the Fair. The children could, no doubt, be made a very attractive feature. The matter will be carefully taken up at the proper time, and I will advise you fully in regard to the matter.

I am personally familiar with the work of the Association, and have, myself, employed some of the children in professional performances. Again, thanking you for your kindly suggestion.

Yours sincerely,
E.D. Price
NY, NY

Members of the Hall did their utmost to ensure the children's stage appearances were within the borders of the law. At times, the Department of the District Police received complaints from people who believed underage children were being employed. In most cases, a birth certificate was produced to prove a child's age.

The debate over Child Labor Laws was fodder for the daily news. Theater managers had a stake in the bill, for the Dorothea Dix Children offered them an attractive advantage of talent, quick study, and propinquity. The success of a performance was diminished when a much older child or adult played the part of a three- or four-year-old. On the other side, progressive leagues and social reformers latched onto this hot debate. Many associated with these leagues were self-promoting and had little regard for the children's needs.

To arrive at a general opinion of stage children, Mr. Reddy reached out to prominent theatrical people, politicians, organizations, and clergy. The manager of the Castle Square Theatre, Lorin Deland, was one of many theater managers that had a vested interest and was a recipient of the questionnaire.

February 9, 1907

My dear Mr. Deland,

As you know I have recently presented a bill to the Massachusetts Legislature, asking for a revision to permit the children to appear on the stage, under the care and protection of the Association, which is a charitable society, organized for the purpose of caring for and educating stage children and the children of actors.

It has been suggested that I write to a few of the most prominent professional people of good moral standing, asking them if they will answer the following questions, with a view of having their replies read before the Committee.

1. Is it an advantage in the training of a person for the stage that they begin their stage career when a child, and is there an age when you would disapprove of them appearing?

2. What effect has such training on a child during the adolescent period?

3. What is the permanent effect on such a person, morally, physically and mentally?

4. Do you approve of children appearing on the stage under such care and protection as this Association gives, which educates and cares for them and which sees that they are accompanied to the theatres, behind the scenes and home again?

5. How does the physical, mental, and moral condition of stage children compare with that of the ordinary in the same circumstances?

I will be under great obligations to you if you will express your views freely, and will be glad to read anything you have to say outside the scope of these questions which will interest the Committee.

Thanking you for your kindness, I am, yours sincerely,
Thomas F. Reddy
Clerk of the Dorothea Dix Hall Association

Mr. Deland answered him with an invitation to attend a meeting of theatrical managers and present a summary of the bill.

February 12, 1907

My dear Sir,

I have your letter of the 9th, and thank you for writing so fully in regard to the question of theatrical child labor. Our next regular meeting of the Theatrical Managers association does not come until February 28th (two weeks from next Thursday). I shall be very glad to have you present at that meeting, if you would like to attend, and explain to our association just what your bill is and what it will accomplish. Their presence and visible interest in the measure at the first hearing on the bill will no doubt prove quite assistance in its passage.

At a meeting of our association, held last Thursday, a committee was appointed to confer with Judge Brockett, the attorney of the association, and with him, to wait on Governor Guild to take up the matter of theatrical child labor and request of the Governor an interpretation of the present law from the Attorney General. The report of this committee will come up at the next regular meeting.

I am sure we are all very grateful to you for the valuable work you are doing in a direction where we are all more or less handicapped by the present legislation.

Yours very truly,
Lorin Deland

The S.P.C.C. heard about Mr. Reddy's proposed bill through Rev. van Allen and was curious about its impact on stage children.

February 14, 1907

Dear Mr. Reddy,

I enclose a letter which I find on my return from the West, from the S.P.C.C. You can expound the bill much better than I; so I leave to you the making of an appointment with Mr. Carstens over the telephone. Next Monday I am free in the middle of the day, and perhaps we three could get together then. Let me know.

> *Hoping that all will go well, I am, my dear Mr. Reddy, with warm regard,*
>
> *Yours faithfully,*
> *W. van Allen*
> *(Mr. Deland says if you get this association to back you, your bill will go through.)*

The reply was forwarded to Mr. Reddy.

February 9, 1907

> *My dear Sir,*
>
> *Your letter of yesterday regarding the bill presented in behalf of the Dorothea Dix Hall Association has come to me and I have read it with much interest. I should be very glad indeed to talk the whole matter over with you any time that you care to come in.*
>
> *Sincerely yours,*
> *C.C. Carstens*

Arrangements were made to meet—it was crucial for the S.P.C.C. to understand the purpose of the bill.

February 16, 1907

> *My dear Mr. Reddy,*
>
> *I have your note and shall be delighted to come over Monday at twelve. I think that we ought to be able to settle matters, so as to secure the co-operation of our friends the 'S.P.C.C.'*
>
> *Ever yours faithfully,*
> *W. H. van Allen*

The three men met and discussed the merits of the bill. Mr. Carstens was interested and assured them that he would make a full report to the S.P.C.C.

Mr. Reddy enlisted his political friends to keep him informed of the proceedings. He later received an update from one of his contacts,

"Commodore'" Daniel MacDonald, Secretary of the Democratic City Committee, ward 3, of Charlestown.

February 14, 1907

Friend Thomas,

Senator Dixon telephoned me this P.M. that the senatorial committee on Rules had concurred with the House Committee in the admission of your bill. There was some opposition from Senator Mullen of Charlestown, the Commodore succeeded in having the Hon. Senator from Charlestown to yield.

Yours truly,
Daniel MacDonald

Rev. van Allen encouraged Mr. Reddy to contact a well-known clergyman to speak or write on behalf of the bill. Plans for the house warming were shaping up, and the guest list continued to expand.

February 23, 1907

My dear Mr. Reddy,

I am glad all goes well. I go to New York Sunday night for the week, returning Saturday, so I shall not be able to appear if the hearing comes then. If it is delayed into the week after, let me know as soon as you can, and I will do my best to be present.

I scarcely know Mr. Frothingham, and it might be better if you were to send him word of our case, and ask him if he would be willing to favor it. I know that Mr. Beal will gladly come, if you notify him.

Have you set a date for the house warming? I should like to know it as soon as possible, in order to try and get the Bishop. If you set a week and then give him the choice of days in that week, that might be the best way. Believe me dear Mr. Reddy,

Always yours faithfully,
W.H. van Allen

In late February, Mr. Reddy sent out a notice to patrons and subscribers informing them of the move to Columbus Ave.

Dear Friend,

We intend, about March 1st, to move into our new home, 748 Columbus Avenue, Boston. We own this house subject to a mortgage and are anxious to pay off at least a part of this encumbrance as well as to furnish the new house. We are seeking contributions either in cash or furnishings and will be very grateful for anything however small.

Our institution cares for and educates stage children and the children of actors and actresses and is charitable and educational. It is incorporated under the laws of Massachusetts.

In moving into our new quarters it will be necessary for us to have many things in the way of furniture, pictures, books, kitchen utensils, beds and bedding, curtains, etc., etc. From those who do not care to make a cash contribution we will gladly receive any article which we can use and will be most grateful.

If you feel as though you could help this most worthy cause I will be glad to have you fill out and return the enclosed to me or you may forward the same to any member of the committee named below. I take this opportunity, also, of inviting you to visit us after March 1, and see the work we are accomplishing.

Sincerely,
Thomas F. Reddy, Clerk

The thought of a larger home inspired all to work hard. Differences between the women were set aside for a time. Miss Whipple looked forward to a larger private room with a nearby bathroom as well as a spacious rehearsal area.

Amanda and Kate organized, cleaned, and packed for the move down the street, while the children continued their school work and rehearsed with Miss Whipple. A new song entitled "The Ghost of Banjo Coon" was added to the program. This was a racially offensive song, but the version the girls sang was watered down from the original. Unfortunately, this form of entertainment was the norm at that time.

6 | ON A MISSION

Mr. Reddy stayed in contact with judges, lawyers, and anyone who added clout to passage of the bill. He sought out opinions from well-known stage actors, many of whom started their careers as children.

Miss Hattie Williams—an actress, comedienne, and vocalist—started her stage career in Boston, earning the admiration of theatergoers as far away as New York City. Late in February, Mr. Reddy received a letter from Miss Williams in response to his questions about stage children.

Feb 28, 1907

My dear Mr. Reddy,

Thank you so much for including me in your circle of prominent theatrical people and asking for my response to the question about children on the stage. As you know, we are grateful for the existence of The Dorothea Dix Hall and the many talented children that I have personally come to know during the times in which our shows require the presence of child actors.

I am reminded of my dear friend Maude Adams, and her unwavering love for the theater and for the children that are a part of its calling. As you know Maude had appeared on the stage at the tender age of nine months, a fact that has not diminished her sensibilities in the least.

There is not an actress, in the entire stage world, past or present, with so much talent, kindness, caring and fairness for her fellow thespian, especially the young. In her role as "Peter Pan", one can witness her sincere and complete involvement with the stage children and their welfare.

I whole heartily [sic] support your efforts in the passing of your bill, but I do have a concern that there may be dangers in the interpretation. I embrace the fact that the plight of stage children is far different than the unfortunate children that are enslaved in the mill and factory work. We dare not lose sight of the bills and laws that keep this particular group of children's safety and welfare in mind. Alas, much work needs to be done in that area. The stage children are privileged, indeed, to be a part of your organization. Their work is a work of joy, in contrast to the mill and factory children who are employed in jobs that offer little or no joy at all.

I fear that following out of a narrow line of a policy could result in undue consequences if the laws are not adhered to with the utmost sincere effort to keep the welfare of the child in mind. Their moral conduct and values could be in jeopardy if allowed to fall into the wrong hands. Your efforts are sincere, and I applaud you for this daunting undertaking.

It is with all my sincerity that I wish you all the success with your bill. I fully understand your mission and endorse your effort for a fair and reasonable amendment.

Sincerely yours,
Hattie Williams

Miss Williams's friends included those in the theatrical and political world. Mr. Reddy responded sincerely to her endorsement.

March 2, 1907

Dear Miss Williams,

Pray accept my sincere thanks for your very kind letter. I will read it before the Committee and I am sure it will be given great weight and careful consideration. Your beautiful tribute to Miss Adams is well deserved. The three children (principals) in her company attended the school in our house while they played Boston and we supplied about ten children ourselves for her "Peter Pan". She will be naturally in sympathy with our bill.

The fear you express in regard to the danger of following out a narrow line of policy for our Association has, I assure you, no foundation, in fact because we understand and have made a special study of this class of children. We know their needs and requirements and the best methods to employ in handling them and mapping out a line of conduct and living. We understand that in their thought, their training and their living they are in a class of their own, and knowing that, we have made our rules of conduct to meet the condition. We are all people of liberal ideas; even our President who is a clergyman has a great love of the stage and of the work of the children on the stage. I was much interested in your comparison of the work of the children on the stage and those employed in factories and mercantile establishments and this and others reflect your views accord with my own.

I cannot thank you too much for your kindness, I may say that nearly every theatre in Boston has employed our children and that our effort to amend the present laws have received the cordial commendations of all the theatrical managers in the City.

Any Friday afternoon at 4:30 that you would like to meet the children at the house #748 Columbus Ave. Boston we would be pleased to have you and I think you may be assured of a pleasant hour's entertainment.

With cordial regard and esteem,
Very sincerely,
Thomas F. Reddy

Preoccupied with matters of the bill, Mr. Reddy received a reminder from Mrs. Glover about upcoming concert dates. She did not address Miss Whipple in person; instead she used Mr. Reddy to relay her message.

March 6, 1907

Dear Mr. Reddy,

We have two concerts next week, one on the evening of Thursday, Mar. 14, at the Heath School in Brookline, and the other on the afternoon of Friday, Mar. 15, at Mansfield. You will probably need to see that Miss Whipple has the costumes and music unpacked in time, also that there is someone to fill Winkie's place if she is still sick. As the one in Mansfield falls on Dramatic Club day, let me know, please, if you want me to take charge of it while Miss Whipple takes care of the Dramatic Club. As to the one in Brookline, I see no reason why Miss Whipple and I should not go together. I think her attitude in regard to not going in is indeed a very silly one, as the concerts go much better with two in charge than with one, and it is nonsense for either Miss Whipple or me to be getting an assistant from outside when we are both disengaged, because we ought to co-operate.

By-the-way, will you ask her to put the concert engagement book which used to be in the office, either on the office table or in the table drawer, where we can all see it for reference as to enter dates? I haven't seen it since we moved, and I may have a date to enter in it this week. It is the book which I bought "For Office Use" and labeled plainly to that effect.

Will see you Friday at the Club, if not before.

*Yours cordially,
Alice L. Glover*

On Sunday, March 10, the house warming party was held. Rev. van Allen, Mr. Reddy, Miss Whipple, Mrs. Glover, and Mrs. Sharp greeted and mingled with the who's who of Boston society. Those in attendance included the governor, politicians, and clergymen along with scores of actors and actresses, theater managers, and the general public. It was a successful event, a day filled with children, house tours, games, prizes, speeches, refreshments, and, of course, entertainment.

Not long after the house warming, problems with the wording of the bill arose. Mr. Reddy met with Senator Thomas P. Riley to correct anything ambiguous. One concern was that the Hall might be placed in the control of irresponsible people, to which Mr. Reddy recommended adding the following clause: "Provided that the privilege granted to said Association under this act may be suspended at any time by the Governor and Council."

He also recommended adding "or any like charitable association incorporated under the laws of Massachusetts after the Dorothea Dix Hall Association," or omitting the name of the association to read "under the care, custody or control of any charitable association," so as not to be misconstrued as a special legislation. And last, if desired to still limit authority, he recommended this clause be added: "Provided that such corporation must first procure a license from the Board of State Police, who shall have the right to grant or refuse such license."

Additional setbacks occurred, however; a misunderstanding resulted in a missed appointment.

April 2, 1907

My dear Mr. Reddy,

I did not get to my office this morning until 11:30, when I found your letter awaiting me. You did not mention any time for the Tuesday appointment at the Governor's office, but I have just telephoned your clerk and understand that the appointment was for this morning. As it is now close to twelve o'clock I am afraid it is too late for me to be there. I am sorry to disappoint you, but there seems to have been no help for it. If I can speak a word to the Governor personally and assist you in this matter, I will gladly do so.

Yours very truly,
Lorin F. Deland

Undaunted, Mr. Reddy continued to refine the bill. He was kept abreast of concerts with reminders and notes from Mrs. Glover. A woman interested in hiring the children questioned the moral implications in some of the songs, as noted in Mrs. Glover's letter.

April 7, 1907

Dear Mr. Reddy,

The concert at Rockland will take place Thursday, April eleventh, and we leave Boston from the South Station on the 6:13 train. The smaller children were asked for, and they would like the sketch, if possible. It is a fifteen dollar concert, and only four or five are necessary. Four would be enough if the program was arranged rightly, and the house would get a little more out of it. However, that is for you to decide.

By-the-way (this is the joke of the season) a lady with whom I am arranging a concert date, was told by someone that there are many things in our concert that are not proper for children to see or know about, and that the sketch is "full of marital infelicities, and is positively immoral!!!" I have invited the lady to the Dramatic Club next Friday afternoon to see the sketch and judge for herself, so will you please have Winkie and Blanche come and give it, in costume? Also it might be well to let the lady hear "Katy Carney" and the other number, so she may be satisfied that the assertion is entirely false.

I hope you are going to Rockland with us, as we all like to have you accompany us.

*Yours cordially,
Alice L. Glover*

P. S. I understand that Oscar Johnson is playing this week. Now you may feel the same about my receiving his money that you did about Ralph Sardaros, but in consideration of the fact that there is over $200.00 due for board for the Johnsons, I think Oscar's money should be handed to me, with no intimation of where it comes from, simply that it is board money, and I will ask no questions. Anyway, the act is performed in New Hampshire, where I understand the child labor laws are not so strict, and the Johnson's earnings have always been applied to their board by request of their mother.

The curious lady was invited to the dramatic club and viewed several performances. Winkie and Blanche gave the show as requested, and the lady realized that the skit was not "full of marital infelicities, or immoral." She enjoyed the popular "Katy Carney" and was treated to two more numbers, "Rag Time" and "Yankee Doodle." She left the club satisfied and entertained.

The passionate appeal for support of the bill brought out the worst in some people. A complaint was issued by the Federation of Labor against the Frances E. Willard Settlement, a home for young or poor women where job training was provided. It was believed to have come from Mr. Reddy or someone at the Hall.

Miss Caroline Caswell, director of the Frances E. Willard Settlement, also had a group of children under her care and was preparing for an operetta. She was not sure as to who entered the complaint, but mention of the Dorothea Dix people came up in a passing conversation and led her to believe that someone connected with the Hall was involved.

April 23, 1907

Dear Sir,

Your courteous letter of the 20th at hand. We are naturally interested in the passage of the bill to which you refer and which is now before the legislature, but as it has been intimated that you or some representative of the Dorothea Dix Hall Association were the parties who entered the complaint against us, I hardly feel as if I wished to unite with you, unless I know this is not the truth.

Respectfully,
Caroline M. Caswell

Mr. Reddy needed support on all fronts; he wanted his name and the Hall's cleared of untrue accusations.

April 24, 1907

My dear Miss Caswell,

Your note is at hand, and to be frank, Miss Caswell, the complaint did not originate from anyone at The Dorothea Dix Hall Association.

Please remember that my bill will be beneficial to your organization and others like it. We all must band together for the good of this cause. I hope you are able to find out who initiated the complaint so that our good name can be cleared. Please keep me informed as to the outcome of this matter.

Most sincerely,
Thomas F. Reddy

The quandary over the bill was a heated topic found in newspaper editorials across the region. The Frances Willard children's dilemma had caused a stir among the citizens. In a note to Mr. Reddy, Rev. van Allen expressed his thoughts on the controversy.

April 25, 1907

My dear Mr. Reddy,

I am sorry that I was away during so much of the exciting time. I only returned Saturday and find your letters here. Saturday afternoon I had an engagement which prevented my presence at the director's meeting, and I have not heard how things came out; but perhaps it was as well, that I was absent, in view of the necessity laid upon me to observe strict impartiality.

Let me know what settlement was agreed upon. I am rejoiced to hear that our bill is advancing so well, and trust that you may succeed in dissipating the hostility.

> *The case of the Frances Willard Settlement children has called public attention to the absurdity of the present law, and I trust that the Federation of Labor will not continue to oppose.*
> *Believe me, my dear Mr. Reddy, with cordial regard,*

Ever yours faithfully,
W.H. van Allen

The Federation of Labor dropped the complaint, and trust was restored between the two organizations. Due to the loss of valuable rehearsal time, Mr. Reddy offered help with their show.

May 9, 1907

Dear Mr. Reddy,

> *Thank you very much for your kind offer of children for our entertainment but we hope that all of ours will come to the rehearsal on Friday night.*
> *I trust it may be possible for you to attend the operetta as you intend to do. We hope it will be a success although I presume the children will not do as well, since they have not had any rehearsals for two weeks.*
> *Thanking you for your good wishes, I am,*

Sincerely,
Caroline M. Caswell

While much was happening in the public arena, the business of the Hall continued with its daily routine. However, early in May, news of the untimely death of a long-time volunteer reached Mrs. Glover by way of Miss Whipple.

May 9, 1907

My dear Mr. Reddy,

I enclose check for $21.00, which comprises all the contributions I have received for the new house, and includes $10.00 from Miss Frances Starr, $5.00 from Mary Young, $5.00 from Miss Foster, and $1.00 from Miss Manning. I am sorry it isn't more. It seems unnecessary, in a way, to send it to you simply to be returned, but it is all right, if you prefer to do it that way.

Is Mr. McBride willing to wait a little for the balance? There will be enough made out of the summer concerts to settle up, and more.

I wrote you yesterday regarding the concert correspondence, and if you have not received it, let me know, because I went into the drug store to telephone Miss Whipple, and cannot remember whether I laid the letter down there and left it, or whether I posted it.

I suppose you have heard of Mrs. Owens death. I am suffering an attack of the blues in consequence, because hers is the eighth death this winter among people with whom I have been intimately associated for years in various forms of charitable enterprise, to say nothing of a half dozen other deaths of relatives and friends.

I do not feel very well this spring, and the announcement of her death was the last straw. I am pretty nearly ready to give up myself. Miss Whipple told me about it over the telephone. Mrs. Owens is the second among our members to die; I hope there won't be a third.

Yours sincerely,
Alice L. Glover

She stayed home from a meeting held later that week and was informed of the minutes in Mr. Reddy's overview.

May 14, 1907

Dear Mrs. Glover,

I enclose $10.00 more received for house. This will give you $334.62 to pay Mr. McBride, leaving a balance due him of $216.48. Please send it to him as soon as you can, because he has been very kind and patient. Say to him that we will pay the balance a little later on and that Mr. Reddy will see him about it. His address is 169 Lauriat Ave., Dorchester.

Sorry you were not able to come to yesterday's meeting. Trust you are better today. The following new members were elected:

Mr. George Whitehouse
Mrs. Doris Whitehouse
Leland Whipple
Miss A.G. Thayer
Mrs. William Cabot

It was voted that the Printing Committee arrange for printing new note heads with new address and telephone number, and Mr. Fuller will consult you about this.

The use of the Dorchester house by the children was approved. I will explain this to you also when I see you.

The Dramatic and Concert Committee want to make a report for the season at next meeting, and I wish you would furnish me with all the information in regard to concerts held this season for that purpose. I would like particularly this information:

Date
Place concert held
Number of children
Price received
Amount received by house for each concert
Amount paid each child and to whom paid

I would like same information in regard to theatres, etc. Kindly let me have this as soon as possible. A vote was passed yesterday, asking you to do this. The School Committee would also like the following information in regard to school children: the names of all children living outside the house, who attend the school, and the amount received from each and the amount now due from each and the expenses of running school including salary of teacher, &c [etc]. The following vote was also passed:

The Treasurer was instructed hereafter in her monthly report to state more particularly the items for which payments are made, so that the Directors may know just where to economize if possible. She is requested to report specifically the monthly expenses of milk, groceries, and provision and the period covered by these expenditures, and what may be due if anything from the Association. Also in the matter of car fare, what the same are for, so that we may know whether they should be charged to house expenses, school, concerts or theatres, and the same with postage and telephone charges or other expenses.

The Treasurer was instructed to pay the bill of $5.00 for flowers sent by Association for Mrs. Owens funeral. The children's bill for flowers I will pay.

Dr. Chandler moved that hereafter all bills due the Association, especially for children's board, schooling, etc., may be paid at the house and left with the General Manager or with Miss Whipple, who are authorized to give a receipt for same, and the Treasurer shall not be responsible for the money so received until the same is paid over to her by the person receiving the same, and the one to whom the same is first paid is directed to pay the same over to the Treasurer as promptly as may be.

And the Treasurer is instructed to notify the parents or guardians of children that payments may hereafter be made at the house. Dr. Chandler stated that this was the practice in all institutions and that as far as possible all the business of the house should be conducted in the house. His motion was carried.

Sincerely,
Mr. Reddy

Despite his best efforts, Mr. Reddy received disappointing news earlier in the week from Representative Quinn: the bill had not passed. A curt note from the governor followed.

May 10, 1907

Dear Sir,

I should have acknowledged receipt of your communication of the 6th instant before this, but I think Representative Quinn, with whom I have talked about the bill in question, has probably informed you concerning the status of the matter.

Very truly yours,
Curtis Guild, Jr.

This news distressed Mr. Reddy and his supporters, who had spent countless hours on this endeavor. Rev. van Allen expressed his sympathies and frustrations about the interpretation of the law and hoped for passage in the next session.

May 21, 1907

My dear Mr. Reddy,

I am sorry that all your labor has gone for naught so far as this year's session is concerned; but it seems plain that next year the matter will be brought up with more general understanding of what is involved; meantime, your suggestion of a test case is excellent, and you are quite right in requiring the managers to meet all legal expenses of such a case. I should like to know how the authorities reconcile their attitude toward our children by allowing Edith Speare, who is only thirteen, to play in "The Prince Chap". There seems no uniformity in their interpretation of the law, as a very good article in the Transcript pointed out a week or so ago.

Thank you very much, in the name of all our friends, for you continued generosity. It is a very gracious thing of you to put the Dorchester house at the service of the children this summer, and I am sure that all appreciate it fully.

What we should do without you is a grave question, and so long as you are at the helm, I think we shall all feel safe.

I wish that I could be at the House, Friday, but I am out of town three days this week on business and do not return until late Friday night. I shall make a point of getting up to the house in a few days, if not this afternoon, as I shall try to do.

Believe me, dear Mr. Reddy, with cordial regard,

Always yours faithfully,
W.H. van Allen

P.S. I have just come from the house: Splendid! All seemed well, except the dietary, which must be remedied. On the east side, a gate is required where there is a wired and picket fence, as the garbage man can't get there. Garbage has been heaping for over a fortnight uncollected, on that account.

7 | TUG OF WAR

It was decided by the dramatic committee that a second concert group was needed to generate more income. Mrs. Sharp involved herself with this new undertaking and shared the task with Mrs. Glover. Miss Whipple was aided by Mrs. Hipwell, mother of the stage child Helena.

That summer was uncomfortable; sidewalks, cobbled stones, and brick houses absorbed the suffocating heat. Fortunately, the concert groups were spared the scorching temperatures, and for them life on the tour was good.

A week after the death of her friend, Mrs. Glover sent her theater and school reports to Mr. Reddy.

June 5, 1907

Dear Mr. Reddy,

I enclose theatre account, made out in same way as I made concert account. If there is anything not clear, I will be glad to explain it. As far as possible I have put down expenses, which were mainly car fares, although once or twice they include "make-up" and several times lunches, which were extra expense to the house on account of Miss Whipple staying down town between shows.

Whenever Miss Whipple kept an itemized account of whose performance she attended, I took her car fares from that persons' account; for example, if 4 children were playing at the Castle Sq. and her car fares were one dollar for that week, I divided it among the 4, each paying a quarter, which lessened the expenses for the house. I think it should be done that way, or else we will frequently pay out more than we get.

I will give you the school account on Friday.

Hastily,
A.L.G.

The next day, as requested, she sent in the school report.

June 6, 1907

Dear Mr. Reddy,

I enclose school report, which I hope is clear. You see by that, if all the tuition is paid, the school will be self-supporting, with $22.17 over, which would purchase more supplies.

I think we should be more strict another season about collecting the money in advance each term, and refuse to let any child enter who is in arrears.

I enclose also the letter from the Children Aid Society, which we used last year to obtain a reduction in fares for the concert trips.

Yours sincerely,
Alice L. Glover

Mrs. Glover did not approve of Miss Whipple making business decisions on her own. She reminded Mr. Reddy of their previous conversation and pointed out that Miss Whipple had overstepped her bounds.

June 16, 1907

Dear Mr. Reddy,

I am sending out notices for dues this month, and Miss Caroline Derby writes in response to hers, that she will be unable to continue her subscription, so her name can be removed from the list of members.

By the way, I believe you and I had a conversation not long ago concerning the lowest concert price, and you agreed with me that we shouldn't go out less than six dollars, in order that the house should make $2.00, the same as the children and that would allow us to send 2 children and give 3 numbers, one fourth of the regular concert.

Did you ever tell Miss Whipple your decision? I ask because I heard her tell a man from Atlantic yesterday that for $5.00 we would send two or three children and give 4 numbers, which is an unfair *proportion, considering that we send only 6 for $20.00 and give 12 numbers.*

I still think that Miss Whipple is not sufficiently business like to make concert prices and arrangements and that it belongs to you and me to do that sort of thing. It is business and does not, according to the by-laws, come under the Dramatic Instructor's duties, but belongs in the Dramatic Committee and the business manager. What do you think about it?

The man with whom she made these terms was a stranger who called at the house trying to get us to give him a hours' work for five dollars, because his church is poor, and as an inducement, he said we would get considerable advertising out of it, but as Atlantic is not a very big place and the church he represents is nearly dead, I do not think it would help us much and we must not establish precedent. The man's wife will let us know later if she wants us.

Will you tell Miss Whipple not to make any engagements for more than one child, under $6.00?

Sincerely,
Alice Glover

All the complaints from Mrs. Glover didn't stop Miss Whipple from getting on with her work and filling her calendar with summer concerts.

July 15, 1907

Dear Mr. Reddy,

I am booking my company through July and August as fast as I can, but perhaps Mrs. Sharp will lay off with her company during Old Home Week. I don't think there will be anything doing for the children though, in Boston.

In some of the small towns there might, where there are no places of amusement. We go to the Rockmere Inn Wednesday night the 17th; Mrs. Sharp said you wanted to go there.

The concert in Falmouth was a great success and every number on the program was received well and I heard no complaining anywhere. Everyone enjoyed the trip and we are hired again for next season which proves the satisfaction of the people.

Very sincerely,
Nella Whipple

Mr. Reddy sent a letter that contained the scheduled performances of the two concert groups to Rev. van Allen and received a grateful response.

July 18, 1907

My dear Mr. Reddy,

Thank you very much for your letter with two concert announcements. I wish I might be present at one of the performances: but my summer travels take me in-land this year. We are spending a few days here by the Jersey Coast and go away Saturday. I should think the double company would be a good idea in every way. Success to it.

Give my love to the children, all of them: and believe me, dear Mr. Reddy, with cordial regard,

Always yours,
W.H. van Allen

Miss Whipple's letter described the welcome received at the hotel. She reported on the revenue and a mix up with a clown suit, closing with an assessment of Mrs. Sharp's abilities.

July 23, 1907

My dear Mr. Reddy,

We were welcomed with open arms as usual at the Grand View last night, concert lasted just 1 hour and 10 minutes, including collection and when it runs more smoothly still will not last much more than an hour without collection which takes more or less time according to size of audience. Collection last night was $14.56 against $12.75 last year.

I hope there will be gain in all hotels. A High School teacher from Philadelphia told me it was the best entertainment given by children he ever saw. Several asked me where I got the numbers etc. which tells the whole story of success.

Mrs. Hipwell had Stella's clown suit along with her. She did not know the others were going out so soon. I am sending it this morning by mail to Adams St. Hope they receive it in time for Wednesday night.

I will make a copy of "The Property Baby" today and send it. I think that is all that they haven't got.

I am writing today to The Preston, Ocean House Swampscott, the York Hotel & the Wentworth, all on our route and some whom we spoke to last year.

Is Mrs. Sharp going to Kennebunk Maine? I ought to know her route so that we may not collide. She knows mine I wish I could have had Mary Greene with me, had I known that Mrs. Sharp did not want her, I would have taken her. She felt badly as she had let another thing slide by to go.

Mrs. Sharp ought to be successful; she has a nice way, as a rule, in meeting strangers and is a good beggar. She can beat me in that. I am no good at soliciting anything.

Sincerely,
Nella Whipple

Miss Whipple considered Mrs. Sharp green and was not happy competing with her group. She continued to send her reports to Mr. Reddy.

July 24, 1907

My dear Mr. Reddy,

We received $29.85 last night against $41.00, last year. Hotel Magnolia is only half full of guests this season. Hotel business is not rushing here, one is closed and the Hesperus, where we go tonight, they tell me has very few guests. Perhaps those few may be generous, we will hope for the best.

Everyone says they like this years' program better than last year's which is encouraging. The children are having a delightful time. Our route has been changed, we are this week:

Tonight—Hesperus
Thursday-Moorlands
Friday—Rockaway
Saturday—not yet booked

> Monday—Hawthorne Inn
> Tuesday—Nanepashemet
> Wednesday—Oceanside
>
> Saturday is hard to book, usually it is hop night. I hope the other company will do well tonight, not much money there, but a good place for the first concert.
>
> New Magnolia Hotel 23rd
> Oceanside 24th
> Moorlands 25th
> Hesperus 27th
> Hawthorne Inn 29th
>
> Our other dates are:
>
> Grand View Annisquam tonight
> Nanepashemet, Marblehead Neck, July 30
>
> I received your letter and will keep you posted, Mr. Blake would like the Atlantic House date July 26th.
>
> Sincerely,
> Nella Whipple

Occasionally, Mr. Reddy would attend a concert to observe the performance and offer his critique. He jotted notes on the side of a program, such as "Too fast," "Too slow," "Not loud enough," or "Replace Helen with Ruth."

The girls would eagerly await his visits. They adored him, competed for his attention, and affectionately called him "Daddy," an endearment that remained with him throughout his life.

After attending the concert at the Oceanside, Mr. Reddy posted his critique and request for information about a couple of girls.

> July 25, 1907
>
> My dear Miss Whipple,
>
> I have received your glowing reports of successes, but I must note that there are inconsistencies in the routines. Your group seemed to be "off" when compared with Mrs. Sharp's company. The Oceanside program

lacked timing and the dance routine was not in good form, making the children appear green. Do you and Mrs. Sharp put in equal amount of rehearsal time? You are our star instructor, Miss Whipple, and I expect the best from you.

Also the lack of communication between departments and parents needs to be addressed; thankfully the other group received the costumes and materials in time for their program.

I am curious as to what happened to the little pianist and Mary Greene?

Please keep me up to date on the two companies and anything else you wish to report to me. Let me know if you are having any problems handling the children, Miss Whipple. I know I can always rely on you to keep me informed as to what is going on during these tours.

I hope you are well.

Sincerely,
T.F.R

A bit of news here, Miss Whipple. I have found out that Irene Martin has signed a one-year contract with Keith's Theater. She is very excited to start her tour. I have often entertained the thought of having a children's theatre someday. What do you think of that Miss Whipple?

Miss Whipple was clearly annoyed by Mr. Reddy's observation of the show. Her response was cutting.

July 26, 1907

My dear Mr. Reddy,

We took at the Hesperus $19.84 against $18.84 last year and at the Moorlands $40.00 against $33.80 last season.

In reply to your letter received last night, I have had far better companies with me than this year. I have only 2 children that I consider up to the mark, Ruth Francis and Catherine McGregor. The others, I have to constantly ding at in order to have them do well. Grace & Edna are both a great care and Edna's cough grates on the audience. I am unable to say whether it is whooping cough or just a bronchial cold. She does not whoop, but expect she will someday and then she will have to go home.

I used to take the children to the Children' Hospital until stopped one year by a contagious disease, afterwards I did not resume it, as *my friend who was superintendent died. It used to be one of my homes. I lived there eight months and for a long time spent Sundays there, so it is quite familiar to me.*

When we first began to rehearse Mrs. Sharp said one day that she wouldn't go out with the children. I said, well if you are not, I will take Clarice with me, for a small child, while attractive, excites too much pity and criticism as to one so young appearing in public every night. Then I should have arranged the parts differently, but now Winkie is taught and Edna is a better size for her, and besides the company has gotten used to each other and work together, unless Edna develops whooping cough. I will keep her.

Mrs. Sharp told me in the beginning that she preferred the big girls and she decidedly said she did not want Helena, would not take Grace and would not be bothered with Edna.

The little pianist I have not with me nor do I think of taking her on any trip unless near Boston, and then only because she wants to go. I told her mother it was too late. Mrs. Sharp saw her at Rockmere Inn and we both thought her too young to depend upon for a pianist. I left her address at the house or would send it to you that you might use her if you wish.

I do not know what you mean by green children, the only real green one in the bunch is Edna. All the others have done more or less concert work. When I started out all were green children, not even used to the public, though no one thinks about that time now.

Did you or Mrs. Sharp ever hear me say I could not handle any child? I know of none that I cannot handle that come to our house. What I did say was that I would not take Vera anywhere with me to stay overnight again. She knows why.

We have not been to a hotel yet that they have not asked for Vera. Ruth, who was with us so many seasons until last, and whom we thought she would be missed, was only asked for once I think on the whole tour. Both Mrs. Glover and I remarked about it. It shows that style makes an impression. Very few of those who have seen us year after year remember Ruth, until I tell them. Strange isn't it?

I think about the coolest thing that has ever been proposed or even hinted at to me is the fact that I do not step forward and give up my route to another, I have worked hard, harder probably than anyone else ever will, walking miles to save car fares, building slowly but surely toward the now successful concert route. How easy it is now for someone else to step in and take it up and coolly expect me to begin over again.

As to rehearsing, again I say that Mrs. Sharp's children were rehearsed equally with mine until the last day when I rehearsed hers alone. All you have to do is to ask the children themselves. Remember please, that the piano player probably threw the children all off. It's what I should have expected to happen.

As to costumes and music, Mrs. Sharp went through both twice with me. I bought the overalls and offered to get pajamas but she said no, she would make pink ones and see to the rest herself.

The music, she took a list of, and said she was going to get it that afternoon. I did bring in a book from home with one song in it that I feared she could not get. I saw to all my costumes and planned them for her, cut out all uniforms & worked like a slave, and under the same strain you all are now. I am glad Mrs. Glover thinks she can bring the children to a satisfactory standard after I have done all the hard grinding work. No doubt she will be entitled to all the praise and will gladly take all the credit.

Irene Martin talks well, but I should believe the contract if I saw it, nothing else. As to Mary Greene, both you and Mrs. Sharp asked me to write to her and Mrs. Sharp used to frequently ask if I had heard from her. When I did, I told her & told her also that she would commence to practice with the children.

She has had more experience than Mrs. Glover and plays for the children better. She has been concert touring with me several seasons. First as a concert child the last as pianist and assistant. Is a pretty girl and popular everywhere. All this I have told Mrs. Sharp. I never would have believed, had anyone told me, that she would treat anyone as rudely as she did Mary. All the children noticed it and Mary felt so badly that her eyes filled with tears and her first impression of Mrs. Sharp is pretty bad. It was all the more cutting because I had told Mary she was pleasant and she would like her. I cannot be so sure again.

I have often talked of a Southern Concert tour and would like to take the children on one but hotel proprietors are not very encouraging about it. They say money would be plenty but that it would all be eaten up by expenses and the hotels are far apart.

As to a Children's Theatre under the existing laws, I doubt it would be successful. The theory is good, but I fear not practical.

I did ask Mrs. Sharp to get the Ocean House & Preston House for me if she could and I did not send letters, though written, there thinking on second thought I had better wait until I knew whether she went there or not. We have been to both. The Preston once, the next season they closed down on all entertainments. I did not try again. The

Ocean House we go to just about as we happen to find the state of mind of the proprietor. The reason we did not stay at Spring Lake last year was on account of an engagement in Peterborough. There are only enough big hotels in this vicinity of Boston to keep one company busy and I tell you all one thing; that Mrs. Sharp did not begin to labor under the disadvantages I did when I commenced. In the first place, she has a pleasing personality and would make an impression and get what she asked for much more readily than I could. In the second place, I was entirely alone, pianist, teacher, costumer everything and no one to consult or go to, no matter what happened or how much I might want to. It would have been just as well, perhaps better, had I done nothing for the other company. The appreciation could not have been less. I have learned a lasting lesson and found that faithful hard work is a thankless job, when given gratis. If I would, like a slave or a dog change my plans every time anyone had a whim it would or might please the whimsical, but the results would not be so pleasing.

Why is it that everyone seems to want my trade, so to speak, the one thing that I have made by my own brain and the labor of my own hands, the success that it is.

The needs of the house is someone to care for the children etc. I can cope with the concert work, but I do not feel like going back over the same ground for the sake of others getting experience. They can do that after I am gone, if they are not willing to learn from me.

If my hard work, my self-sacrifice brings me only slurs and knocks and if I must submit the best to others, keep any old thing myself, knock about any old way etc., I at least feel that I deserve the merits of my best work, the one thing that I am adapted for and have made successful, the one thing that I should govern.

Others can rule the house and children much better than I, but as yet there is no one in the Association who can do my work in the concerts. I do not say there are not others who can. I know there are, but most of them who have developed the talent as I have, draw large salaries.

You wrote plainly to me and I have answered plainly to you. It is better that we understand each other.

I feel sure Mrs. Sharp will make a success of what she undertakes of the company. Since the change, I have not seen, but they are capable of good work. I would not take Mary in my company under any consideration. She is too young. Edna at 7 is young enough, beside Mary has whooping cough which if anyone ever knew would score heavily against everyone, besides she is always car sick everywhere she goes.

We play the Surfside Saturday night.

Now that we have had it out, so to speak, I think the least said about the two companies the better and each of us try our best to do what we can and quit wrangling. I for one am tired of it. The idea of my consulting any one as to the children's concert ability is rather laughable to me, considering there is no one who knows their ability, their short comings and their worth as I do.

Very sincerely,
Nella Whipple

Miss Whipple, obsessed with her signature work, feared that the other women would seize it from her. The lack of respect began to take its toll. It was the first season using two companies, and she was unaccustomed to being compared with anyone, especially someone like Mrs. Sharp.

Aug 3, 1907

Dear Miss Whipple,

Now that we have two companies on the road, I must say that I am very pleased to see that Mrs. Sharp's girls did an exceedingly good job at their performance. I think she has done an excellent job of teaching the girls their routines, don't you agree Miss Whipple? We are fortunate to have her take charge and earn more revenue for the Hall.

What happened to Helen Hancock? Why was she not at the concert?

I realize that you are working with green children and that it does take time and patience. I hope your stamina will keep up during this season, Miss Whipple.

On another note, it puzzles me to have heard that you have been critical of the behavior of Mrs. Sharp's group. As far as I have witnessed they are well behaved and seem to enjoy being with Mrs. Sharp.

Please remember, Miss Whipple that the addition of the other group is a benefit to our home and to the children themselves. We need cooperation between the two. I trust your concerts will go as well as hers. You are the professional, Miss Whipple.

I expect to see your weekly statement by the end of the week.

Sincerely,
Thomas F. Reddy

P.S. It looks as if we still owe $11.00 for some props. Could you look into this?

Infuriated by Mr. Reddy's letter, Miss Whipple responded by opening a floodgate of bitter resentments, complaining that her hard work had been dismissed as others reaped its rewards.

Aug 5, 1907

My dear Mr. Reddy,

Your letter received. As usual you have several wrong impressions. In the first place every one of the children you have selected, with the exception of Helen Hancock, have been taught by me, and Helen Hancock has seen the children do Santa Claus & Banjo Coon and many other things several times and children are cleverer at imitation then [sic] original work. With Mrs. Sharp's company to teach them, they will imitate. Edith Witham & Blanche Winters came to me entirely green. Blanche, I do not consider very good. Clarice is new, Florence last year was very green, and perhaps she has worked into the spirit of things by this time.

Helen Hancock, I sent word to about the concerts, I think by Doris Horslin or Allison Black. Word came back to me that her mother would not let her go. It would perhaps be wiser if you did not swallow so much talk without finding out the truth of matters.

I did not know that Mrs. Sharp was going with the children Thursday, so as to insinuating anything as to their behavior with her was wrongly interpreted. I thought she had engagements elsewhere.

Because I, with my own brain, my hard work have made the concerts the success they are, the one prominent and successful thing of the house. Like other things of success, there are plenty to grab it. It does not seem to occur to anyone, except a few old friends of the house who have grown with it, that the scheme is not to do for the house and children that gets along any old way, but the desire is to grasp the concert work away from me. That is the interesting part, and never mind if I did build it up. It must be taken from me that others may enjoy it in its fullness and perfection. It is a pretty toy and amusing, though it is mine, I have nothing to say. Why? Because I will not be a slave, an underling, a servant to those who know nothing about the work, but who insist on forcing their way without listening to wisdom gained by experience. It is always there they tell me; whenever a new superintendent comes to an organization, the same old ground must be gone over while he gets experience.

I do not claim to be always right, I have always been open to suggestions. Had I not, I could not have been successful, but I do resent insults, and the fact that I must be pushed one side. Let things go as they will. I wish to have no more to say. I will go on with my little concert company. We will do the best we can, fulfill our engagements, renew old friendships and make new. I do not work with a desire to beat anyone. I do not care one way or the other. You probably would not allow an assistant in your law office to walk off with your practice, gained by years of labor; doubtless you would resent it to the last. I know my work, my audience. When the Association was formed it was to help the house, the children, leaving the dramatic work to me, but now nothing seems to be mine. It makes me feel that had not my sacrifice proved its worth, that failing would have been kinder. It takes much patience to work with green children, a practiced eye and intuition to see beyond their greenness something attainable. All were green when I started. Fifteen years the children have been banded together and now the new members catch the spirit quickly from the older ones.

It is not true that most of the children come to us with their talents well developed, some do, more now than in years gone by, but even their talents are not always developed in the right way.

Words go very little ways with me, the proof is the success, the warm welcome, the renewed attention summer after summer. One can always call up words from friends to fit their point of view. Last year the children did look seedy, but that was not my fault, there have been seasons when they have looked better than this. I am sorry you feel you must object and resist any effort put forth by me. You play to win, you have told me often. You are able to do it.

I have given my all away, the best years of my life also, the thanks are insults and the desire to make me a slave, but, I fear that I was born to rule, and therefore do not accept slavery very gracefully. My particular kingdom has been, is still the dramatic work, but I have made up my mind to resist no longer. There is a right and wrong to everything, and justice, though often tardy, comes sometime and I will bide that time. You must expect me to work with disheartened interest after so much quarreling, so many insulting insinuations, and so much ungratefulness. There is nothing more to be said. You go your way, I go mine, which I suppose is the end, the future way. The house, the children boarding here, of course I have nothing to do with, it is not a part of my work now. They may and do need more or less attention, but my work is with the dramatic children, with these I will work, sending you weekly statements, just as Mrs. Glover does.

Sincerely,
Nella Whipple

[P.S.] The $11.00 Amanda says was never paid. I sent her money for bills, she had enough for all but this. No bill was sent us and I had eventually forgotten it. It must be 3 or 4 years ago. It seems he called once or twice the next season, but I was away. It slipped both our minds until called up by your letter.

The next day, she sent a short note absent the anguish revealed in the previous letter.

August 6, 1907

My dear Mr. Reddy,

I was just about to start for the Children's Aid Society when your letter came. It saved me the trip, for which I am much obliged.
 We went to the Lincoln House, Swampscott last night, tonight to Colonial Arms, Gloucester. Thursday night we go via Fall River Line to N.Y. If I remember right, we had to give time, place and rail road to the Society. So I write you that you may be able to tell them, if they ask.
 Our Casino Concert in Spring Lake is Friday night and I think Saturday afternoon also.

Sincerely,
Nella Whipple

8 | PLAYING WITH FIRE

In August, both concert groups were based at the Cliff House in Maine. They often stayed at the same hotel before leaving on their separate routes. This arrangement allowed group rates and gave the girls time to be together.

While at the Cliff House, Mrs. Sharp wrote to Mr. Reddy all the news of their stay. Unlike the other women, her relationship with Mr. Reddy was flirtatious and edgy. She was comfortable engaging in playful banter with the reserved man. She wrote daily and became upset when he was slow to respond.

August 8, 1907

My dear Mr. Reddy,

We arrived safely and have just finished the performance, and the collection was $26.98, is that all right dear? The people are simply wild about the children and they are as good as gold, no trouble. They have put up some cots and things in their parlor for us, so we could stay here. It is much better than going outside. I am going to see the other hotels here (2) tomorrow and try for next week. There is also a casino and they want us to give an entertainment there next week if we cannot get the hotel, but we will see later.

If you cannot read this, don't blame me, as there are about one hundred strangers asking questions, and as many faces, but the only face I want to see is absent. The children all want to send you cards so you will probably get some mail in a day or so.

A gentleman on the train wanted to know if they were all my children and who their father was. I told him he was on Court St. Boston, he was an old man, so that is excuse enough.

The Madame will have to keep busy if she wants to dress in this place, as the ladies go beautifully gowned, but I care not, I simply want their money and make good for you, dear. Do come down Friday,

I want you. I will write tomorrow eve after the performance. It was the best show they have given, all snap and go. I hope things will be all right with you tomorrow.

Good night, and pleasant dreams dear, until Friday.
With cordial good wishes,

Always sincerely,
AVS

[P.S.] The Madame has just whispered to me that she cannot help flirting. Too bad, I am better employed writing to you dear, it gives me more pleasure anyway.

Mrs. Sharp's animosity toward Miss Whipple was evident. In contrast, her relationship with Mrs. Glover was a cool, polite alliance. They had their own disputes but managed to sort them out in a civil manner.

August 12, 1907

My dear Mr. Reddy,

We have just finished the concert at the Sea Shore and the collection was $10.83. Can you imagine a thing like that in such a place?

The master of ceremonies is one of those icebergs that thinks he is doing you a favor to look at you, but he changed his mind before the evening was over and wants us to come back on Monday evening, which we will do if nothing better comes up. He says they will know us then and things will be better. We expect to get the Lawrence for tomorrow eve.

After you left this morning I went to "Bay View" with the posters and over to the "Orchard House" to see that everything was all right. I asked Madam to go and see the Sea Shore man while I was gone, as Bay View is 25 minutes ride from here, and do you think she went? No sir. When I got back at 2:30 she was telling the story of her life in the sun parlor. So I went to the Sea Shore myself and got it.

The man at the Old Orchard House is the most charming man one would meet in this work, understands all about it and is much interested and wants to see the children. He is a dramatic and dancing teacher in New York so I want things pretty well up for Wednesday Eve. He thinks we will do well, I hope so, as I am afraid you will get disgusted, but it is not because I do not try, have been at it all day and am up writing this so you will get the news as soon as possible. Don't worry dearest, we will come out all right if I don't die soon. It is just as lonesome as can be here tonight. I miss you very very very much, that is more than you can say truthfully.

I taught Mazie "I Am Bad" this afternoon and she did it tonight. That got them warmed up early. She was great. They applauded her again and again. Of course the Madame will say she taught her but I don't care as long as we get the money.

Things are going very smoothly, no trouble or complaining. I had Juliette's dress washed today so she would have it clean for tonight and the children looked nice and clean. They are getting very popular around here now, as everyone is beginning to know them. I wrote to Cliff House Kennebunkport today to see if we could get a return for their Sat eve—Aug 24—as we go to Oceans' the 26—and they are both together and it is country and quiet, so if we do not see you this week will you come down there, please dear, as I am just as lonesome as I can be. I am sending with this a copy of them. The children are as good as gold. I took Juliette with me this morning. You are always sure of her—good manners, etc. I got some things for Allison with the money you so kindly gave me and she is very grateful. She will write tomorrow, also Doris.

Mayor Fritz is at the Old Orchard and will be on Wed. eve. Mr. Lovely said he would have him at our show. I have just heard from the Summit Spring House—(you know the circular you gave me in the office when you were here) saying we could have the twenty seventh or eighth. I will write tomorrow and take one date.

Mrs. Glover is writing to hubby and giving him a good call down saying he is not the only pebble on the beach. Old Orchard is full of them. I know a pebble I would not change for all the pebbles in the ocean, but he would change me for any kind of an old shell, would you dear? I hope you will enjoy your rest at New Salem. I know you want to see the children and Mrs. Glover, more than that I dare not expect, but there is someone else who wants very much to see you. I will write you every day so you will know how we are and do try and find time to send me a line as often as you can, you know what a neglected mortal I am.

> *It is after 11 and I am dead tired so will say good night dear and many many good wishes from the last and only. Come down soon.*
>
> *Very sincerely,*
> *Annie V. Sharp*

At times, Mrs. Sharp's profits were considerably lower than Miss Whipple's. This troubled her as well as Mr. Reddy. Her letter from Old Orchard Beach called up reasons for Miss Whipple's success in Spring Lake. She believed it unfair to compare the two companies.

August 13, 1907

My dear Mr. Reddy,

Your letter of this morning has certainly discouraged me. I really think under the circumstances that it is unkind to make any comparisons, as far as Miss Whipple is concerned. I don't believe one word of the Spring Lake affair. She would tell any kind of lie and so would Mr. Lackery, if they knew we would hear it, and again, Miss Whipple has been there for four years with the same people, where down this way they do not even know the children. I am only surprised that a clever man like you are, would believe any of their yarns.

I will finish what dates we have here which will bring us up to almost the first of Sept, then we will come home and perhaps you would be better pleased to have Miss Whipple do Atlantic City, as I am beginning to think Miss Whipple is right, concert work etc., is not in my line, try as hard as I can. I am an impossible woman and my sister after all, is right.

They were telling me here last evening that we would do well at the Old Orchard house. I hope so.

As far as Atlantic City is concerned, there is so much doing outside it may be very cold inside, but I am sure Miss Whipple could make a fortune there. I certainly would not tell the children, as I have too much consideration for their feelings and they are working hard and doing their best, as we all are.

I am glad you are going to New Salem. Hope you will have a good rest. We will not have any off days, as we intend to work every night.

I have not heard from the Poland Spring House regarding the exact date but will look for a letter tomorrow. Perhaps there, where there are no other attractions, the no-goods will make good.

You see dear, at Spring Lake there is no attraction and the cottages are all very wealthy people interested in children, and if after four years they did not do swelling, it would seem strange. I gave your letter to Mrs. Glover to read, but did not say a word to the girls, just gave them your love as you asked me to.

I am more than disappointed at the thought of not seeing you until Sept, but you know best what you want to do, and of course what I want or think is no difference, and much as I would like to see you it will have to wait. The weather continues the same as when you were here and I hope to have it so for the remainder of our stay. We are going to Cliff House Saturday eve. 24th and I know we will do well there. When you look things over quietly, what does Miss W. do outside of Spring Lake? The collections are no larger than ours have been.

I am very, very sorry that I came at all and only wish I had stayed at home. I am glad you are sending Margaret with "Uncle Tom." They need the money, why doesn't Eva go?

I am not surprised to hear you have not heard from Miss Whipple, she does as she pleases and goes right along. You see, she pay no attention to the order that she was to report every day.

I hope to have better news for you tomorrow eve. I will write you after the concert.

I told Mrs. Glover she must rehearse the children every afternoon so they would not get careless, but she loves to air herself, so it is hard to get her to work, but she did yesterday afternoon. The children are going into the hall tonight. Mr. Mikelsky wants them. He said last night that there was a cheap crowd here and at the Seashore, but the Fiske and Old Orchard were different. I hope so for your sake.

There is no news dear, things are just as you left them.

With love from the children and many good wishes to you dear always.

Sincerely,
Annie V. Sharp

Mr. Reddy sent help whenever a production needed extra stage children. This gave the girls an opportunity to expand their experience with popular shows such as *Uncle Tom's Cabin* or *Peter Pan*.

After a visit to Old Orchard, Mr. Reddy took one of the girls back to Boston for another engagement. On the ride back, they talked about the concerts, the other girls, and Mrs. Sharp.

August 13, 1907

Dear Mrs. Sharp,

I have taken the liberty of booking your concerts in Atlantic City. I know you and the children want to go there.

I have also written several letters of introduction. I did so in light of the fact that you seem to have lost some of the momentum that you had processed at the start of the season.

I hope that you will recover quickly and get on with the show, so to speak. I am also hoping that your collections in the next few weeks will be an improvement over the last few concerts. We don't want to fall behind in that area.

Mrs. Sharp, I do hope you allow the children some fun time, on their own. All work and no play is not good for anyone, especially young children. I am sure you agree, Mrs. Sharp. We must strike a balance between being strict and lenient, or children will lose respect and rebel.

I trust you are feeling better, Mrs. Sharp. I will look for your report in the post.

Sincerely,
Thomas F. Reddy

Grateful for his help, but curious as to what was said to Vera on the ride home, Mrs. Sharp responded promptly.

August 14, 1907

My dear Mr. Reddy,

Many thanks for your book of Atlantic City, also for the writing of the letters. It was more than kind of you to do it when you are so busy and I am truly grateful to you for your many, many kindnesses.

What did Vera have to say on the way home? Your letter of yesterday had such a very, very cold tone I could not understand it, as I am unconscious of doing anything to call for more than usual ice.

There were four strangers came up to me yesterday and complimented me on the behavior of the girls, said they never saw anything like it, no one calling or yelling at them as it is usually the case with a crowd like this.

Mrs. Glover went for the Lawrence last eve, but could not get it, so she took the "Aldire," the collection was small but helped out on expenses, while waiting for the others.

If Atlantic City is half as good as it looks we will bring you back thousands, as you say, but it is hard to get the attention inside when there is so much going on outside, but I am willing to try anything for you dear.

I thought by the cold chill of your letter yesterday you were disgusted with me because I could not make more money for you.

Your friend Locke has just been here telling me how foolish I am to write letters only, not dictate them as he does, he is a wonder.

The children went to the ball last eve, had a great time. Doris wore her Quaker suit, Stella her clown and Juliette her Dutch with wooden shoes.

Allison, Edith & Mazie we kept with us, did not let them on the floor.

This place is full of the freshest men I ever saw. They think because you happen to be in concert work that they can say anything they please to you.

I wish you were here dear, but then I always want you every place with me. Hope you are having a good rest. Write me dear, as often as you have time, as the days seem doubly long when I don't hear from you.

With love from all and many, many good wishes.

Very sincerely,
Annie V. Sharp

She later sent a note to update Mr. Reddy on the amount collected at the Old Orchard House. It showed that her revenue had improved.

August 14, 1907

My dear Mr. Reddy,

We have just returned from the Old Orchard House. The collection was $25.75. The guests were simply wild over the children, pelted them with flowers and all that sort of things. We go back there Saturday afternoon at 3:30 for a matinee and they asked me if they could make up a purse for us and I thought you would not mind, so I said yes, unless they cool off before Saturday we will get more money.

> I wrote to you today but I knew you would be interested to learn this. No letter from you today dear, what is wrong? Are you forgetting me? I am afraid I will have to get Mrs. Glover to scold you.
>
> Will write tomorrow eve after the concert. Much love from all to you dearest, always.
>
> Sincerely,
> AVS

Mr. Reddy would often leave a gift for the girls when he visited them. Doris Horslin was pleased with the gift he left and sent this note of thanks.

> August 14, 1907
>
> Dear Mr. Reddy,
>
> I received the little jumping jack that you left for me & thought it was fine.
>
> All the girls and Mrs. Sharp and Mrs. Glover are in the sun parlor. Allison was very pleased with her present & asked me to thank you for it. There was a Masquerade last night and Mrs. Sharp and Mrs. Glover and Juliette and Stella and I all went. Juliette wore a Dutch suit & Stella her clown suit and I wore my Quaker suit. We had a fine time.
>
> We are all well and I hope you are the same. Well I must close now with x-x-x.
>
> Your "best boy,"
> Doris

He also received a thank you note from Alison Black.

> August 14, 1907
>
> Dear Mr. Reddy,
>
> I received your present for my birthday and thank you very much and hope someday I will know your birthday so as I can give you something. I thank you very much.
>
> Yours truly,
> Alison

P.S. Are you coming down?

Mrs. Sharp and Mrs. Glover remained in Maine while Miss Whipple left for Spring Lake. There, the head matron enjoyed financial success at the hotels and casinos. She was clever at her game.

Thursday, August 15, was like any other warm, breezy day on Old Orchard Beach. Mrs. Sharp, Mrs. Glover, and the girls left their hotel, the Emerson, to enjoy the late afternoon air before their next performance. But in a few short hours, a fire consumed most of the Old Orchard Beach's boardwalk. According to the *Daily Kennebec Journal,* it started in the annex of the Olympia House and was fanned by a brisk southwest wind, destroying a block of wooden buildings that housed stores along the boardwalk.[2] The fire then spread across the Boston & Maine railroad tracks and devastated a crowded district of hotels, boarding houses, and cottages. This event was reported from Maine to New York and beyond. It became known as the "Great Fire of Old Orchard Beach."

All the girls were safe, but their costumes and personal belongings, left at the hotel, were destroyed. The group relocated to the Bay View, and Mrs. Sharp sent a brief description of the fire without dwelling on the disaster.

August 16, 1907

My dear Mr. Reddy,

We have just returned from Old Orchard, had to come back here as there are no accommodation at the beach.

People are sleeping outside on the beach and they are running special trains every 15 minutes to get the people away, the only hotel left is the Old Orchard, all the rest of the beach, from the depot to the Sea Side Park, is in ashes.

We give our matinee at the Old Orchard tomorrow at 3:30 and hope to do well, we also give another concert here tonight as we only took $7.16 last eve, they all went up to the fire, so will not lose a chance to make money.

So glad you had our reply from Atlantic City. The master of ceremonies at the Old Orchard told me to go and see Prof. Dawson at Young's Pier and use his name and the Prof. would do all he could for us.

---

2. "Summer Hotels on Fire," *Daily Kennebec Journal*, August 15, 1907.

> There was [sic] more questions asked around the beach last eve, about the Dorothea Dix party than anything else, everybody seemed to be curious about us and almost everyone we met this morning stopped us, we have made ourselves quite popular by our good behavior, which I know will please you dear.
> We are coming home tomorrow eve after the matinee as we have lost all our clothes and cannot go along any further until we go back and get clean clothes.
> You may write me at River Court upon receipt of this. I thought we could fill our date around Boston and then go to Kennebunkport Saturday and Monday then to Summit Springs and Poland Springs, then back home and to Atlantic City.
> Try and keep Tuesday evening for me dear, so I can see you when you get home from New Salem and we can talk it over and I will do just as you say, as you are always right. I will keep all the news dearest until I see you which I hope will be very soon. With much love from all to you dear.
>
> Very sincerely,
> Annie V. Sharp
>
> [P.S.] Did not pay to stay over for Sea Side Park as it is dead here everyone is looking and thinking about the fire.

The group quickly regained their composure, as if the fire were nothing more than a distraction. On August 16, one of Mrs. Sharp's girls sent a note about the fire.

> My dear Mr. Reddy,
>
> I received your letter day before yesterday & was more than pleased that you thought enough of me to write.
> I suppose Mrs. Sharp has told you all the news of the fire. We could only get the Herald but I suppose that the other papers told lots of lies about it. They are charging 54¢ for the Herald, imagine that. Must close now, as Mrs. Sharp is waiting to mail this.
>
> With lots of love, in haste.
> From Juliette

Miss Whipple was in Spring Lake and did not learn of the fire until a few days later.

Aug 18, 1907

My dear Mr. Reddy,

Enclosed is order for $46.45. The last three nights here have been Carnival nights & days, so that the receipts are not very good.

Last night was a grand finale, with fireworks etc., so there were only a few elderly people left in the hotel. I thought it best to do what we could rather than lay off.

It looks now as if we would go to York, Maine, Monday the 26th for 3 days only, then to Bethlehem—children are well and everything is all right.

Sincerely,
Nella Whipple

[P.S.] Did you get last weeks' money all right? Have had no acknowledgement.

She sent a request for more posters, but by this time the excitement of the fire had faded—the resilient girls had moved on to new places and songs.

August 22, 1907

Dear Mr. Reddy,

I think we had better take some more posters with us.

About the tickets: We shall go to Bethlehem someday next week. If you get the tickets I can have them dated afterwards I think, unless you can get them good for any date during Aug. and Sept.

Will not know positively about York until I get to Boston. They may have no open date next week. If not, will go directly to the Mountains, as York does not amount to very much, and probably, expenses and all considered we might make it up in the mountains.

Only have written to the 3 largest hotels in York. We have some new hotels in the mountains that we wrote to last year who promised us a date this season.

I am sorry to learn that the other company were in a fire. They must have had an exciting time of it. I take it for granted no one was hurt.

Our children are well. They receive too much attention that both mine and nearly all their time is occupied with present people and affairs.

A privilege and a blessing of childhood.

Sincerely,
Nella Whipple

9 | A MIXED MAILBAG

The fall brought changes in schedules, increased enrollment, and new instructors. Mr. Reddy sent notices to parents interested in enrolling their children at the Hall.

Dear Friend,

Your attention is called to the opening, for the season of 1907-08 of our private school for stage children and the children of actors, which takes place on next Monday, September 23, AT 9:30 A.M.

The school this year will be in charge of a new teacher of experience and in every way qualified to perform the duties involved. It is our intention to increase the efficiency of the school and to place it on a par with the best public and private schools in the city. The course will include the primary and grammar school courses, with special courses in studies which will be of benefit to stage children such as vocal music and voice culture. The tuition is $15.00 per year. The school hours are 9:30 to 1 every week day except Saturday and Sunday, with the usual holiday vacations. The Dramatic and Concert Committee has decided not to use any children in the theatres except those who attend the school in this house.

Those who contemplate joining must send in their names at once to Thos. F. Reddy, 42 Court St., Boston, Mass, as the number of pupils will be limited and we intend to take only as many as our school can comfortably accommodate. Please reply without delay, stating your name in full (stage name, if any) age, stage experience, parents' names and any other information which will be of interest.

Yours truly,
Thomas F. Reddy, Mrs. Annie V. Sharp, Mrs. Edward Wade, committee

> *P.S. The Children's Dramatic Club meetings begin Friday, September 27, 1907 at 4 P.M. and continue every Friday at the same hour for the season. Be sure and attend the first meeting.*

Letters continued to flow in from potential students and parents interested in placing their little ones in the care of the Hall. Actress Ellie Palmer needed a place for her child. She traveled with different productions and found it difficult to take her along.

> *August 25, 1907*
>
> *Dear Mr. Reddy,*
>
> *If convenient for you, I should be pleased to call tomorrow (Monday) about two with my little daughter, Queen, and go through the Dorothea Dix home as I wish to place her there next week. I am liable to go on the road at any time, but may be in town a week longer.*
>
> *She seems delighted to go to the Dorothea Dix as I talked and explained it to her. Kindly excuse pencil.*
>
> *Very truly yours,*
> *Ellie D. Palmer*

Queen was enrolled and thrived on the attention she received. Her mother, on the road with *Uncle Tom's Cabin*, inquired about the welfare of her child.

> *Sept 22, 1907*
>
> *Dear Mr. Reddy,*
>
> *I am at present with the same show which May and Marge Lawless are with and like quite well.*
>
> *Of course I can do better later on, but we play cities and the best theaters, even if it is a Tom show. My mother will call and settle Queen's board and then I will send it every week.*

If it is not too much trouble will you kindly let me know how my baby is and if she is well? Tell her I send my love to her. We are doing good business. Today I stopped at Philadelphia and enjoyed it very much.

Kindest regard to all at the house & to yourself

Truly yours,
Ellie D. Palmer
Stetson Uncle Tom Co. Will play York next Thurs. That is in Penn.

She was happy to receive a response from Mr. Reddy about her little daughter.

Sept 30, 1907

Dear Mr. Reddy,

Thank you very much for writing me in regard to my little Queen. I am very happy to know that she is contented and well. As I am a little short this week, will send you $6.00 next week for her board. They kept back part of my salary. I am not going to stay with this show as I have a better offer and I go to Philadelphia next Sunday so in case of necessity you will kindly write there Gen[eral] Delivery.

We play Hagerstown, MD Wednesday and Reading Penn next Saturday. The other towns I did not get as yet.

Excuse haste.

Very sincerely,
Ellie D. Palmer

[P.S.] May & Marge send love to you.

However, her financial situation was unstable, and when shows ended or she left, it took time to meet Queen's expenses.

October 8, 1907

Dear Mr. Reddy,

I wrote you last week that I would send some money for Queen's board but as I am laying off this week also been very sick will be obliged to ask you to wait another week. Thanking you for all your kindness. I hope to be able to work next week.

Give her my love and tell her mama never forgets her.

Kind regards to you and all the folks and especially Mrs. Sharp & Miss Whipple.

Sincerely,
Ellie D. Palmer

Mr. Reddy kept Miss Palmer informed of Queen's progress. As always, she delighted in the care her daughter received.

Oct 14, 1907

Dear Mr. Reddy,

I thank you very much for the kind interest you have in little Queen and I shall never be able to repay you for the same. I rec'd a letter from you yesterday telling me of her success with Miss Bates and it pleases me very much.

I am feeling a little better today and expecting a message to leave town, but some of the managers are so slow.

Give my little darling girl my love & tell her when mama gets to work she will send her something nice. I never forget her, but know she is in the best possible place with the association. Kind regards to all & especially to you.

I remain, sincerely yours,
Ellie D. Palmer

The summer season was nearing its end. Mrs. Sharp continued to keep Mr. Reddy up to date on the concert tour and was curious about a prospective new hire.

Sept 3, 1907

My dear Mr. Reddy,

Yours of Monday just received, I'm so glad to hear from you. I wrote you two letters Sunday which I hope you have received this eve. The concert tonight as far as the work was concerned was very good, but the collection was $5.18.

My dear, this is the cheapest place you ever got into. The Wiltshire was a very cheap sporty place, simple people, you know.

This is a city of hotels, true enough, but then there is only one in just about 6 in the whole place that are fit to go to. The others fill in.

The man at the Ostend has been more than kind. He gave me a letter today and I called on them. Got the Savoy tomorrow eve, by almost getting down on my knees to them.

They don't want any entertainment; the guests at the hotels are very insulting. You would think we were, I don't know what, but if we could get the money I would not mind that part of it.

The man on the pier was away, will not be home until tomorrow, when I might see him and the other hotels. You learn to wait hours to see people. They are so busy and have so little time to spread around with any one, but we talked one hour to the manager of the Chelsea and then he said he would think it over.

It is the worst ever, and unless I can fill up some dates tomorrow I think it would be a waste of money to stay around here and pay out what we have. The man at Rockmere was right.

Mrs. Glovers' sister is the most profane person I have ever met and I wish she would go home. I don't think it is a good thing to have her around the children, she is too loud and course. I know you think I am a crank but I don't approve of women swearing and it is not a good thing for the children to hear and I have told her good and proper that I would not stand for it.

It has been raining some here today and the people are leaving. The hotels, a great many of them, I mean, are closing up. If we can get some of the places tomorrow it will help out, but men here put a penny in the hat and think nothing of it. Boston men are good enough for me. I always loathe these New Yorkers anyway and the more I see of them the worse it gets.

I hope to see you Thursday and I am more than sorry to have to write as I do, but it is the truth. I don't think this place is good for anything. You might just as well go to the hotels in Revere, just the same, on a larger scale.

What has Mrs. Glover to do with you getting a teacher, I would like to know!

The children are like panicky, they are anxious to see you. If you were here you would understand many things that seem impossible to you, now don't get discouraged, I am not a bit so, and things will come out right, they always do.

Be good and don't forget your family who are out in the cold world trying to make a living. Good night dear and much love to you from all xxxxxxx. These are your good night kisses.

Sincerely,
Annie V. Sharp

The setback from the Old Orchard fire resulted in heavy losses for those involved. Mr. Reddy enlisted help from Rev. van Allen to find a way to ease the burden of the deficit.

Sept 3, 1907

Dear Rev. van Allen,

It is impossible at this time of the year to get a quorum for a meeting of the Board of Directors, but the only matters of importance are these; we should appoint a school teacher for the coming season, and as Chairman of the school committee I advertised for one, and have interviewed one that I think would be satisfactory. Do you approve of leaving the matter of the selection of the school teacher to the School Committee or the house?

The other matter is the loss sustained by the concert children in the fire at Old Orchard Beach, where these children were performing at the time of the recent conflagration, and lost everything they had with the exception of the clothing they wore at the time. Mrs. Glover and Mrs. Sharp were with the children at the time and they lost everything also. As these people were giving their services to the Association for nothing, I have been trying to think of some means of making their loss good. The only things that occur to me are soliciting subscriptions, and when the children return from the concerts, to give a benefit concert for the children. I will be glad to receive any other suggestions.

I am sending a letter similar to this to each member of the Board of Directors.

Yours very sincerely,
T.F. Reddy

Rev. van Allen sent out an appeal for subscriptions to help with the expenses for the home and belongings lost in the fire.

September 6, 1907

Dear Sir,

Enclosed please find a booklet describing the work of the Dorothea Dix Hall Association. We trust you will read it and then join with us in this useful benevolence.

At the present time money is much needed for the following purposes:

First: Three hundred dollars at once to send the house children to the country. This year we have sent them to the summer camp of the Girls' Friendly Society at New Ipswich, N. H., under the charge of Rev. W. H. Prescott and Miss M. L. Schirmer.

Second: The mortgage on our house is now due and the executor of the estate holding it has notified us that we will have to replace the mortgage. We should very much like to reduce it at that time, as the interest on the present amount is a serious drain on our treasury.

Subscriptions should be sent to Dehon Blake, Treasurer, 27 Kirby Street, Boston, and marked for either of the above purposes, or for the general expenses of the home, and they will be gratefully acknowledged by him.

William Harman van Allen, President

Although numerous letters of praise, such as Ellie Palmer's, were received, not everyone shared that attitude. One parent vented his frustration about the condition of his little ones. Mr. Wilson Frank (his stage name), an actor in an English travesty group, was not pleased with the level of care his children received or the management of the school. Added to his claim, several of his letters had gone unanswered.

Oct 15, 1907

Mrs. Sharp,

We were very surprised to find our dear little ones in such poor condition when we went for them on Sunday and think it very poor management on your part not letting Amanda know that we were coming to take them for the day, had I not written to Mrs. Regan, they wouldn't have known anything about it. And another thing, I've written you on several occasions and you've not answered one of my letters. If it had not been for the kindness of Mrs. Glover we should have known nothing of our little dears.

It was very different last year when Mrs. Glover was Manager and Treasurer, we knew all about them.

Poor little Winnie was quite ill so we left her at home to be nursed and again, having her vaccinated without our consent was a great liberty to take, and then to send them to a public school, when they were supposed to be taught at the Hall. Learning there at the Hall was the main idea, so that they would not have to go out in all kinds of weather, besides going without an escort, I think that is a very poor way to send little children out. I might say I feel like expressing my feelings to the Board of Directors as I am sure if they knew of the existing conditions they would not tolerate them, but think of the little ones comforts who they have pledged their selves to look after. I do not expect to send our little dears to school again as it seems other people do not think of their comforts. Regretting I have to make these complaints.

I am yours truly,
Wilson Franks

Mr. Reddy replied to justify a few points that were misjudged. Mr. Franks was on the road for weeks—sometimes months—at a time, resulting in misunderstandings.

October 20, 1907

Dear Mr. Franks,

It was with interest that I read your recent letter addressed to Mrs. Sharp. I am not sure what it is that you consider to be 'poor condition.' We at the school and home take the health of our children very seriously. Winnie was ill, a stomach upset, and at the time you and your wife were on the road. We tried on numerous occasions to reach you. As far as your objection to the vaccination, it was determined by our house doctor, Dr. Chandler, that Winnie had not been vaccinated for small pox. Also, I might remind you, that when you left the children in our change, you agreed that it would be up to the house doctor to prescribe or administer medical services if needed, and as he sees fit, in the event of being unable to reach you.

I would also like to point out that we are going through a transition with the school session, at this point, and we are in the process of hiring another teacher. We felt that until she was in place that the public school was the best answer for some of the children. Your children and two others attended the public school for a short time. The school, by the way, is just down the street and they were always in the company of the older children.

With all that is done for your children, I find your statements ungrateful and unjust.

Sincerely,
Thomas F. Reddy

The response was brusque.

Oct 25, 1907

Dear Sir,

Your letter at hand and contents carefully noted.
I shall take pleasure in calling on you one morning next week and saying before you actual facts to prove to you we are neither ungrateful nor unjust.

Yours sincerely,
Wilson Franks (Frank Wilson)

Soon after, Mr. Franks removed his children from the school. It is not known if he took them on tour with him or left them in the care of others. The Hall was the only charity that offered that care. Another option would have been a convent.

In appreciation for help at an event, Mrs. Sharp sent money to Alison Black's mother. She received a letter of thanks in return and shared it with Mr. Reddy, noting that gratitude was seldom received from anyone at the Hall. By this time, the terms "Daddy" and "Mother" had sidled into her letters. It was the children's notion that they needed a "Mother" to go along with their "Daddy."

Oct 24, 1907

"Daddy" dear,

This letter is worth framing, at least it is to me. Really dear, it is the first word of thanks or gratitude I have received from anyone in the D.D.H. So you see it does pay in some cases, and when we least expect it from. I am so glad I got it for her.

I missed your voice on the phone today. I am on my way to the Hollis St Theatre.

Wish you were with me dear. Will see you tomorrow.

Sincerely,
"Mother"

Included was Mrs. Black's thank-you note.

Oct 24, 1907

My Dear Mrs. Sharp,

I must write you these few lines to thank you for the $5.00.

I almost dropped dead on the moment. Alison spoke to me on her return, when she said you sent me $5.00. I thank you so very much. I cannot express my feelings on this paper. You may guess when I expected about .50 cents. I hope I may be able to serve you in some way again. I thank you a thousand times.

Yours truly,
Mrs. J.G. Black

It was the end of another busy year. The popularity of the children's work continued to grow as child labor debates dominated the press. Mr. Reddy took care of the necessary paper work to keep the concerts in line with the law.

As in years past, another successful Children's Christmas Party was given. Mr. Reddy once again made sure that each child enjoyed the festivities and wonderful gifts provided by him and others. The next year held a lot of promise and change for the children, the Hall, and Miss Whipple.

PART THREE

CONCERT

BY THE

Dorothea Dix Children

AT

Huntington Chambers Hall

ON

Saturday, February 20, 1909

AT 2.30 P. M.

INCLUDING A NEW SKETCH
ARRANGED BY

JOHN BEACH

FROM STEVENSON'S POEMS ENTITLED

"BY THE FIRESIDE"

WITH INCIDENTAL MUSIC

The Dorothea Dix Hall, a home and school for stage children and children of Actors is located at 748 Columbus Ave., Boston.

10 | HIT OR MISS

The dramatic committee proposed a benefit concert to help cover the financial losses from the fire. The girls worked on the hit of the year, "Yama Yama Man," a spooky song and dance routine that they loved just as much as the audience.

A polished performance demanded concerted efforts from each of the women. Miss Whipple prepared the children for the show, keeping them in line with her bell whenever they misbehaved, and Mrs. Glover managed to gather a medley of sheet music for the musical director.

January 12, 1908

Dear Mr. Reddy,

Replying to yours of the eleventh, I do not know how the musical director is to procure copies of all we are to use at the benefit, I have partial orchestrations for "Yankee Doodle Tune" and "A Frangesa" (Stella's dance) but they are only for violin, cello and cornet, and I suppose he wants them for full orchestra. Mr. Poole, however, has Stella's dance, "A Frangesa" for he told me so at the Christmas party, and no doubt he would lend it. Helen's dance is "Cupids Garden" and Mr. Hipwell has the orchestration for that, which he will lend us. The "Banjo Coon" I have in full and "Captain Willie Brown" can be procured of Mr. Marshall at Remicks on Tremont Row. "Holsteins Band" is published by Ditson, and the orchestration can probably be obtained there. All of the numbers are in the key of Db except "Banjo Coon" which is in G. If there is anything you don't understand, I will explain when I see you Monday afternoon.

In haste,
Alice Glover

While Mrs. Glover worked out the kinks with the sheet music and Miss Whipple rehearsed the children, Mrs. Sharp dealt with the costumes and stage mothers. When a favor was asked by Mrs. Black, she handed the request off to Mr. Reddy.

January 30, 1908

Dearest "Daddy",

The enclosed will explain itself. I have answered her saying you had charge of that department.
    Hope to see you soon—I am getting lonesome.

Fondly,
"Mother"

Alison's mother had her daughter's best interest in mind.

January 29, 1908

My dear Mrs. Sharp,

Alison said the Concert Children are to give a concert at the Church of the Advent Monday night. Mrs. Sharp, being Alison is a member of the Sunday school there and there is a number of the young men there who know Alison, would you favor me by placing Alison a little prominent in the concert numbers, as I want them to think Alison is improving in her work. You understand how I feel in regards to it and her being one of their Sunday school children. I think it would be pleasing to all of them who would know her.
    I hope you won't feel angry towards me for asking this and I do hope it is in your power to do this for me. Please thank Mr. Reddy for the pay Alison received Tuesday Eve. As that was her first pay concert at the D.D.H. and you may be sure she and I were more than pleased over it. Thanking you for all past favors I remain,

Yours sincerely,
Mrs. J. G. Black

The benefit was held on February 3, 1908. It was a wild success. "Yama Yama Man" brought the house down, as did "Yankee Doodle Tune" and dancer Stella Craig's performance. As for Alison, Mr. Reddy made sure she was placed front and center.

Entertainments given by the girls usually elicited positive reviews from the audience. However, the next concert produced concern from one spectator's viewpoint; his report to Rev. van Allen was not flattering.

Feb 13, 1908

Dear van Allen,

I went over to the Sailors' Haven Concert on Monday night and saw the Dorothea Dix children take part in the performance. I have had much experience in club work, and have learned not to expect too high a standard, to make allowances and all that, but it seemed to me what those children did, and the way in which they did it, cannot fail to be disastrous to them. Then too there were the late hours, I doubt if they got home before eleven—and the crowd of rough sailors. We would not think of subjecting our own children to such an experience, and I don't quite see why we should aid and abet other peoples' children in it. I say "we" advisedly because it was "Trinity Night" at the Haven and we "put on" the Dix children and so we are "participating criminals" if crime there is.

Don't feel that this needs an answer, but think the matter over. I suppose the Home depends partly upon the earnings of the children in giving these shows, and that complicates the problem. Money has an eternal fashion of complicating problems, when it does not make them.

R. Kidner

The Sailor's Haven was a home for men recently discharged from the Navy. It was under the direction of the Episcopal City Mission and not the best place for children to appear.

Whatever the performance was that evening, it did not meet the approval of Rev. Kidner. The crowd was rough, as described in the letter, and weather played a part in the late show. Future shows were limited to a more civil crowd.

11 | ADD AND SUBTRACT

The Hall hired another instructor in response to increased enrollment. The search had begun in the summer of 1907 and resulted in dozens of inquiries and applications for the position, such as this one:

Dear Sir,

I saw your advertisement for a teacher for a private school in the Boston Transcript. I feel that I can offer what you seem to need. I am a college graduate (Tufts A.B.) and hold a Boston H.B. certificate. I have had several years' experience in high school work, but am looking for private school work and would be glad to take a place even if the salary were low to get into that line of work. I have a thorough musical training, including pipe organ theory, piano and the normal music course (public school music) and have had much experience in drilling children for one sort of performance and another. I should prefer not to board at the school, if it were possible arrange it. I shall be pleased to receive further information and will meet any plan for an interview you may suggest.

Yours sincerely,
(Miss) Lucie M. Gardner
Salem, Mass

Miss Lucie Gardner was offered the position and accepted it. She was an attractive young woman from a well-respected family in Salem, Massachusetts. Her role included assisting Mrs. Sharp and Mrs. Glover as pianist for the summer tours.

February 2, 1908

Dear Sir:

I have thought the matter over carefully and have decided to take the school. Hope the arrangement may be satisfactory and the result advantageous for the children.

It would accommodate me very much however, if I might defer beginning the work until Feb. 17. That would give her two weeks' notice and would make it possible for me to finish the present term and get past the examinations before making any change in hours.

Kindly let me know if this is satisfactory at your earliest convenience.

Yours sincerely,
Lucie M. Gardner

The reputation of the Hall and the children flourished; everyone knew who they were and respected their work. But, in some cases, unscrupulous parents claimed they were members of Dorothea Dix Hall to gain theatrical parts on behalf of their children. Mr. Reddy identified the problem and sent a letter to theater managers to remind them of the importance of using the original Dorothea Dix children.

My dear Sir:

At the opening of another Theatrical Season we beg to call your attention by way of a reminder that for many years this association has supplied the stage children for the theaters in Boston when children are needed. We have with us this year a larger number of clever children than ever before in the history of the organization.

The children that we send are all professionals, of experience and if the selection is left with us, as it usually is, we invariably pick the one who is best qualified to play the part.

The supplying of children for theaters has always been a financial loss to our Association as there is more or less expense attached to it and we are encouraged to undertake this work in the interest of the children and as part of their education.

We use no public school children at all. All that we furnish attend the private school in our house; the hours of which are managed so as not interfere with their stage duties.

We have several children who are particularly "quick studies" and who are sent in emergency cases where a regular child employed in a company is suddenly taken ill or leaves without notice. The fact that a child can be thus procured at almost an instants notice has a ton of material benefit to theatrical managers and one which they fully appreciate by their kindness from the Association and then good words for our work.

It sometimes happens, however, that a manager in his dilemma forgets our Association & therefore I moved to suggest that the envelope card be placed in a convenient place where it will serve as a reminder or perhaps save you much trouble and annoyance.

It sometimes happens that children (though more often their parents) personally solicit engagement at the theaters and represent themselves as connected with this house. Sometimes they are, but more often they are children we cannot recommend and perhaps are such as should ever be selected and more often are children whose education is being neglected by their work in the theaters.

This Association looks after the moral and educational welfare of stage children and you can therefore render a great service to the work of our Institution and be sure of always procuring the best children by dealing directly with our house and not with the children or their parents.

May we ask for your cooperation in the good work we are doing for stage children by your promise to aid us in this matter?

With best wishes for a successful season.

Yours very sincerely,
Thomas F. Reddy

> *Copies to:*
> *Bowdoin Sq. Theatre*
> *Orpheum Theatre*
> *Boston Theatre*
> *Keith's Theatre*
> *Colonial Theatre*
> *Majestic Theatre*
> *Hollis St. Theatre*
> *Park Theatre & Tremont Theatre*

By April, Miss Whipple had reached her limit. The unpleasantness continued between her and the other women. She resigned her post and left her beloved Dorothea Dix Hall with a promise to the children to stop and visit whenever she was in town. She took her few belongings—her dated wardrobe, books, sheet music, photos, and costumes—and convinced Amanda and two boys to relocate with her in New York City.

There, she rekindled old friendships, started the "Actor's Child League," and established a fund for care of needy children. Within a month she was ready to take her inexperienced ragamuffins on their first summer concert tour.

12 | FULL SPEED AHEAD

The summer tour was in full swing. Mrs. Glover and Mrs. Sharp made their way along the coast and enjoyed the hospitality offered by the hotel managers. The departure of Miss Whipple was a relief to the women, although the older girls maintained a sense of loyalty for the woman who had cared for them for so many years.

The letters posted during the summer of 1908 were filled with information about the hotels, guests, children, revenue collections, and run-ins with the former head matron. Mrs. Glover wrote of business and gossip, whereas Mrs. Sharp continued to bare her thoughts on her abilities, her misgivings, and her desire to be with Mr. Reddy. She and her group left Poland Springs for the Cliff House in Kennebunkport, Maine, and arrived in unpleasant weather. The behavior of a few of the girls had become disruptive.

July 14, 1908

"Daddy" dear,

We are here again from Poland—It is raining torrents and Rye Beach, as you saw it dear, is an Atlantic City compared with this place. We took $24.26.

Oh dear, I am so anxious to make money I am getting nervous. The business is very bad all around here, very few guests at the hotel. I hope we will make it up in August.

Your card saying you were coming made me so happy dear and then your letter saying you were not coming made me blue and homesick. We all want you to come dear, I in particular, but that will not bring you. I know you would not come to see me, but Mrs. Glover will be here. I will get her to write and ask you.

The children are working well, but Julie, oh heavens, she is the meanest ever, just keeps quarrels going all the time, begins them just before the concerts. The two Ruth's are the cards and of course that makes Julie angry. If she had played fair we would have gotten $75. At Poland I sent Ruth and Julia in the room and Doris in the office and outside—Doris got about $4 in change and Julie on one side of the hall got about $8. So you can imagine how I felt when they came in, but Ruth Francis came in with her basket full and turned on Julia like a wildcat saying "Why didn't you go to everyone" and that made a fuss but it put me on in a minute and you bet Miss Juliette goes on no more collections. She started in today to ruin things but changed her mind. I made a few kind remarks and now things are fairly pleasant.

Saw Miss Gardner. She will tell you how nicely everyone along the line has treated us and I think she will probably tell you a few other things besides.

Ruth Francis is going to stay home when we return the 30th so we will have to arrange things, not because of her boyfriend, Timmy S. he is away, but for other things. I think Blake is too fresh and I don't blame Mrs. Glover one bit. Lucky for Blake he did not send me a letter like that. They make more money—but such is life, it really doesn't pay to try, who cares, they think you are wrong any way.

Ruth Fielding is doing a little better, but she is the hardest one, but you need her in the concerts, so I will put up with anything as long as you want these trouble makers.

You had better change your mind and join us next week—I want so much to see you—Will look for a letter tomorrow. With love and kisses from the children—

Sincerely,
A.V.S.

The poor collection from three days of concerts disappointed Mrs. Sharp as much as the antagonistic behavior of a few girls.

July 17, 1908

Dearest "Daddy",

We have just finished our concert and I am disappointed—the collection was $58.32 and I wanted to do better but my luck does not run that way, but perhaps my hot air friend at the Wentworth will save the day—

Mr. Cushing and the guest have been kindness itself to us, and the children made good. Ruth Francis was the hit all around before after and during the show. She got all the money.

Julia is just as nasty as she can be. She makes no effort to do anything but make trouble. She had Ruth Francis crying nearly all during the show just because they don't pay attention to her, and Stella, the fool, follows along like a poodle.

Mr. Cushing called me into his office at supper time and told me I had some well-behaved girls with me and he had a large table set up in the extreme end of the guest dining room and made me take the girls there instead of the children's dining room. He said it would be a good "ad" to have them walk in and out. I was thinking how swell your handsome pianist, Miss Lucie G., of the other company would look walking the full length of this dining hall with her bathing suit walk and evening dress. I have not had a line from you, never mind "I will remember that".

I hope things will clear up. I will tell you all the news when I come home for I don't suppose you will come down, but I miss you and want to see you. Hope you are having a good rest.

With much love from all,

Fondly,
"Mother"

As Mrs. Glover prepared Mrs. Hipwell to take charge of her group while in Maine, she emphasized that Miss Whipple had arrived in Gloucester—along with a former Dorothea Dix student.

July 18, 1908

Dear Mr. Reddy,

I have some news for you. The "old woman" is in Gloucester! She came down today on the morning boat, with Ralph Santaro. One of the men at the Oceanside said she came over there to make a date and that she was coming with her company in a few days.

We took $32.23 there tonight, the audience was large and enthusiastic, but it was two-thirds "kids" and they never have much money. The children looked well, particularly Gracie & the "Glowworm" and "Rag-time."

I have arranged with Mr. Hyams for next week when they go to Rockport. I have straightened out everything as well as I can for Mrs. Hipwell and have rehearsed the children nearly every day. I hope things go well, but I have my doubts, because Miss Gardner is of no use, except to play the piano, & Mrs. Hipwell will have everything to do. Mrs. Hipwell is not very well pleased with the change. I have told the children to mind her.

Very sincerely,
Alice L. Glover

Another poor concert and sparse collection were noted by Mrs. Sharp. A run-in with Miss Whipple depleted her stamina and opened questions of her being used. Mr. Reddy was with Mrs. Glover, a sign that she was being ignored. She longed to be back in Boston.

July 18, 1908

Dear "Daddy",

Have just finished a very poor concert and a very bad collection $6.63 the meanest ever—

The Madame arrived ahead of us—and was resting when we came. She is as ugly as the devil and I would like better than anything to be in Boston. It is all so discouraging—quarrels and the back biting.

I wonder if any of this crowd is true, or does everybody use me. I will be more than glad when it is all over.

This is such a pretty spot. You can see the sea and the water is almost as pretty as Atlantic City. Of course we will lose money here, but the hotels are half empty. A trip this way before the 25th or later is wasting money, but someone must be the goat. I suppose this condition will continue from now on, poor music, poor concert and poor collection but it will have to end soon.

Mrs. Glover's girls are lucky to have you with them. I feel the chill of it all, letters and everything, but never mind Daddy, someday you will know. With love and kisses from the children,

Sincerely,
"Mother"

Having finally received word from Mr. Reddy, Mrs. Sharp's letter from the Cliff House in Kennebunk was a mix of consternation and repentance.

July 21, 1908

"Daddy" dear,

Thank you so much dear for your letters. I was just about as homesick as could be without a line from you. I will tell you the news when I see you. Ruth Francis has no fault with D.D.H. neither does she know how useful she is. It is Juliet, the whole thing from beginning to end, but I know dear, you will see things as I do when I tell you. Everything is smooth but I am getting nervous prostration keeping it so, but I will, because I want to bring the money home to you.

I am sorry, very sorry that my letter from Prout's Neck was nasty. I did not mean to have it so, but I was so discouraged with the children and everything. If you had been there dear and seen things as I saw them, you could not blame me. We can make some changes before starting out again and remedy all this trouble. I will tell you later dear. The children have sent you cards and letters, I did not tell them to, as I, like yourself, do not like things that way.

I had a letter from Miss Gardner yesterday and she said she would like to finish the season with me. I wish she could. This music is awful. I do not believe anything Mrs. Glover says and the 'being used', did not mean you dear, but the children using me as they do. I know you don't, because I am not much use to anyone. Of course the girls don't like me because I make them mind as I do, but I know you want them well behaved. If we are lucky enough to have you join us I will talk over things then tell you what I would like to have you do, will you do it dear?

Do come down, I want to see you oh so much.

With love from all, fondly,
"Mother"

Mrs. Sharp insisted on good behavior from the girls. When they got out of hand, she would discipline them or take away a special treat. Mr. Reddy did not always agree with her methods of punishment, which led to a lot of her remorseful letters.

July 22, 1908

My dearest "Daddy",

Thank you so much for yours of this morning. It was sweet and kind for you dear to forgive me for what you know I regret. But when the children misbehave and do poor work and I see a losing game dear, I get cross, but you know why, I am over anxious to please you and if things go wrong I just can't stand to see the money going, but I will try and be different—but you know dear, I don't mean you, no matter what I say—

It is raining and lonesome here—and I will be glad if we can get any rooms at York as sleeping on the floor for a week is rather tiresome. Mrs. G. has a room and bed so that keeps her quiet, for myself I don't care. If you knew I wanted to see you very very much would you come down dear? Do please, I want to see my "Daddy" the best and dearest "Daddy" in the world. Do come down.

I don't believe we will do much tonight dear as the place is small, but I will try. I am sorry sorry sorry dear for anything that has seemed nasty—

With much love, I remain yours, a very fond and repentant
"Mother"

Mr. Reddy took a much-needed break in New Salem. He had Doris Horslin and a few others with him. After the July concerts were completed, Mrs. Sharp and the girls returned to the Hall for a short break of their own.

August 3, 1908

"Daddy" dear,

Many thanks for yours of this p.m. I was at the house today and saw the children and Madame. The girls were more than pleasant. I gave Vera two pairs of silk stockings (black & pink) and Blanche a pair of black and blue, telling them they were from you for their birthdays. They were simply wild over them and of course they think "Daddy" is just the best on earth, all of which is true. Probably the next thing, I will be accused of putting high ideas in the children's heads, of silk stockings etc., but I don't mind it, I want them to have good things and refined taste if possible.

I phoned the "Surfside" and found they could not have us until the last of the month, which time of course we cannot fill. I phoned your "Honest to God" friend and he was having a dance and concerts of his own this week so could not give us a date. If you doubt these statements (which I hope you won't) you may call them up. I have Young's for Wednesday evening and the "Ocean View" for Thursday eve. You know the Ocean View, it's the one on this opposite corner from Crest Hall, a new one to us, but perhaps we can get something out of it, at least you cannot accuse me of not trying. I will write the children as you suggest and also Miss Gardner. Mrs. Hipwell was at the house today. She looked well. Later we had a long talk being there alone. She said Miss Whipple did not ask her to go with her. Now, what are you going to believe?

I was talking with the lady I spoke about, regarding her coming to the house and hope to be able to get her, if I can, I will feel all right and it will not seem as if I was deserting the ship, for she is more capable in every way than I am and can help you much. This is all the good news and I don't know of any bad as yet. There will be nothing to bring you home before Monday. I can get along, not as well as when you are with me, but will do the best I can. So do not come home until you are ready. Too bad we cannot have Ruth Fielding for Monday evening, but we can get along all right. Miss Whipple told Catherine that the hotel proprietor told her the program this year was not as good as in the past, it was too old. Such a bunch I never saw.

So glad you are enjoying yourself. So am I. Some friends are here with the K. of P. convention and I am just sporting, but you see I did not neglect the concerts just the same. It is so good to see someone unexpectedly and I also enjoy having them in town. Write me often, it will help to pass the time until I see you.

With much love to Doris and best wishes to you.

Very sincerely,
"Mother"

The confusion with Miss Whipple and her troupe continued. Mrs. Glover described to Mr. Reddy a conversation she had with a woman about the different companies.

August 12, 1908

Dear Mr. Reddy,

While we were waiting for supper at Sugar Hill, a lady came to me and said "I am very glad to see your children again; I saw them at Bass Rocks early in the season. You have had two companies down there." I said, "Yes, the other company is in Gloucester now", to which she replied, "Oh, I mean earlier, the two companies were quite close together. I said "The second company wasn't ours!" "I knew they didn't look like yours, but they said they were Dorothea Dix children, at least, two of them did." Then light dawned on me and I said "Yes, the two boys probably said so", the lady said "Yes, they did. There were two boys & four girls". When I told her that the two boys once lived in our house for a time, but had no connection with us whatever now, she said they ought to be stopped from saying that, because it would hurt us, for she herself wondered how we could send out a second company so inferior to the first. Now what do you think of that? Hasn't that old "she-devil", (excuse strong language) got nerve to have the boys say they are Dorothea Dix children. But it is just like her. Be sure and tell Mother Sharp. Can't we find some means to restrain old Whipple from these things? I expect anytime to see her in Bethlehem, as a man here told us he had had considerable correspondence with her, and she had expected to come, but he didn't know, surely, whether she would or not.
 If I hear anything more, will let you know.

In haste,
Alice Glover

Her next letter brought news of a good entertainment and collection. Some of the guests had remarked about Miss Whipple's absence and how much better the children looked and behaved.

August 13, 1908

Dear Mr. Reddy,

Arrived here yesterday afternoon and gave a <u>very</u> good entertainment, receipts $41.33. Many of the guests liked it much better than last year, and they are all glad that we have a return engagement. Some of them openly expressed their satisfaction that Miss Whipple is no longer with *us. They all spoke of how much better the children look this year, both uniforms and costumes, and two ladies came to me and said that there is a marked improvement in their behavior; they said that last year the children were allowed to run about unattended, and that they were all over the hotel, always in evidence. They were much pleased because the children are never out of my sight, and are behaving so quietly. I never saw them so good and so subdued myself. I am almost afraid to mention it for fear it won't last.*

They have had candy given them this morning, and an auto ride, and tomorrow they are to go in the swimming pool at the Mt. Washington.

The posters were received at Fabyan's all right, and are in place.

We met some of the guests from there this morning and they said everyone is looking forward to the entertainment.

I had a long letter yesterday from Mother Sharp and am glad to hear that her receipts are so good.

I hope the Spring Lake trip will be profitable. I am sure it will be self-supporting anyway, and I am glad you have decided to take it, as it will be well in many ways, even if we only clear expenses.

Will write tomorrow.

Alice Glover

P.S. Our entertainment at the Mt. Washington is advertised in the "Bugle" and on the menus.

The concert at Mt. Washington resulted in success all around. Both Mrs. Glover and Mrs. Hipwell found the amount collected hard to believe; it by far surpassed the previous year's collection under the former head matron, which brought a bit of smug satisfaction.

August 14, 1908

Dear Mr. Reddy,

I suppose you will find what I am going to tell you hard to believe; I had to count the money three times, myself, before I would believe it. Our collect at the New Mt. Washington was $91.98, and the children never gave a better concert in their lives. I told you that Catherine McGregor was popular in the mountains, and I think you will agree with me, when I tell you that she brought in a twenty-dollar bill, two five dollar bills, one two-dollar bill and several ones, and every one *over there was saying "Isn't she cute?" There was sixty-three dollars in bills and twenty-eight dollars in silver with ninety-eight cents left over for the girls. Then someone sent them a dollar for themselves, so they each had thirty-three cents. When Mrs. Hipwell counted the bills and found 63 of them, she was so excited that she hadn't got over trembling when the show was over, and the children are as delighted as we are. After what I said in yesterdays' letter about Helena's dances not taking well, I was much amused to have her get on[e] of the biggest encores of the season at the Mt. Washington. They liked everything, but her dance, the rag-time number, the glow-worm and the sketch were the special favorites.*

As our expenses to Bretton Woods, including our stay there, were only $21.45 and our receipts were $159, not counting the children's money, our net profit was about $138.00, not bad for three performances.

Mr. Anderson had us give the Mt. Washington show this afternoon instead of this evening as he thought we would do better. I will explain when I see you. Judging from receipts, he was right. Won't you please write to the children and tell them you are pleased, for I think they would appreciate a little praise.

The guests came out on the veranda to see us off after the show, which is a great deal for that house, as the people are not enthusiastic there, as a rule.

I wish Old Whipple could know what we did there, for last year she took only $22 in the same place. I hope now that we can beat her at Sunset Hill Monday.

We had a beautiful place to give the concert at the Mt. Washington: there is a lovely stage in the music room, with decorations which showed off our costumes to great advantage. The costumes and uniforms get great praise everywhere, and I am glad of it, for Mrs. Sharp worked so hard over them. The concert itself get lots of compliments both the program and the children's work, & some of the latter I take to myself, for I drilled & rehearsed them faithfully before we came up here, & I have been working with them ever since we came, noting faults each night and correcting them the next day. Considering how we came out at the Mt. Washington, I think you will be wise to heed the manager's advice about postponing the Mt. Pleasant date. I wish we could have another at Crawford's, either the night before or the night after the next Mt. Pleasant.

The manager of the Alpine at Bethlehem has asked me to give him an earlier date than the 27th as he is afraid some of his best people will be gone by then, so I have given him Sat the 22nd. I have filled the four open dates you left me as follows; Thursday Aug. 20 mat Crofts Hall, eve the Columbus. Fri. Aug 21-Sinclair-Sat. Aug 22-Alpine-Mon. Aug 24 Mt. Washington in Bethlehem. The Alpine man says we can have the 27th just the same if we want it, or a later date if we stay after the 29th.

I do hope the Spring Lake people will be generous: a few collections like todays would put us on Easy Street.

The children send love, and say to tell you to come and see us.

*Yours sincerely,
Alice L. Glover*

The competition between the two companies continued along the White Mountain route, but Mrs. Glover remained confident in her abilities.

Aug 20, 1908

Dear Mr. Reddy,

Yours of August 19th just received, and I will be guided by what happens after Miss Whipple and as to whether we stay longer than originally planned. If she interferes with business much it is not worthwhile to stay. As soon as I hear from the Mt. Pleasant, I will let you know. As I told you, Miss Whipple arrives next Monday and so I told the Mr. Pleasant people that we would change their date from August 25 to any date they want between September 1 and 8, provided we can, come ahead of Miss Whipple, but that if they had given her a date next week, then we would prefer to stick to our original date of Aug. 25. I told them why very frankly. I ought to hear from them tomorrow, and then I will let you know. I think perhaps we had better try for the Flume House and the Waumbeck, just to make a start there and some people from No. Conway, who were in Bethlehem for the day, begged us to come over there. If the Mt. Pleasant changes our date, it would be well to take the Twin Mt. House for a matinee the same day, as it is right on the way and we can't lose anything that way. Did you receive the check for $150.00 which I sent you?

The returns for the Crofts Hall matinee today are $24.53 about a dollar less than last year. The returns from the Columbus I will add at the bottom after the show tonight.

If Juliette is with Miss Whipple and is wearing anything of ours, I shall order her to refrain, as I am not going to have any misunderstanding.

> *I am cooking the old lady's goose in every hotel, as fast as I get the chance.*
>
> *In haste—A.L.G.*
> *(Columbus $9.09)*
>
> *P.S. Don't be scared; I am not getting "cold feet" over the old woman! Some people who saw the children this afternoon and who were very friendly with the old trollop last year, came and told me that there is a marked improvement in the children, the uniforms, the costumes and the pianist. (This is the first time I have had any "taffy.") They said the children look as if they had enough to eat this year. This is one reason why it was well to send this company to the mountains, because being practically the same children, the difference is noticeable.*

Another afterthought explained the problem of securing a date with the Uplands. Mrs. Glover offered a suggestion on how to handle the scheduling conflict caused by Miss Whipple.

> *Since writing this letter, I have seen the proprietress of the Uplands, (I told you before she is the only one who hasn't been nice to us), and asked her about the 28th which you have on the list in pencil for a return date. This is the 2nd time I have asked her. Couldn't get any satisfaction the first time and this time she said she couldn't give me an answer till she saw Miss Whipple, who must have the first preference this time. Now if you say so, I will tell her politely that we don't follow Miss Whipple and then I will make another date for Friday, write me so I can get it Monday morning as that is when she told me to call, We only took something like $10.00 at the Uplands and it isn't worth taking insults for, but I will do just as you say.*
>
> *A.L.G.*

Even with paltry returns, the show went on. Mrs. Glover looked for engagements at a few places in the White Mountains and wanted to secure a place at the Waumbek. Much to her annoyance, a few distractions appeared in the form of Mr. Hipwell's arrival and Miss Whipple's sustained trickeries.

Aug 20, 1908

Dear Mr. Reddy,

The collection at the Park View tonight was $10.68, and Mr. Hardy, the proprietor, is highly disgusted because it wasn't twenty. The audience was large and enthusiastic, wildly so at times, and he says they ought to give me twice as much. However, it is six dollars better than last year, at that. Mr. Hardy wants us to try again if we stay after Sept 1. He says he will be glad to see us at any time. He told me tonight that Old Whipple is coming next Monday, and has taken rooms over Goodale's Photo Studios, on the main street. Goodale told him so today. He asked me who she had with her and I told him. He seemed astonished when I said she tried to get our children and failed.

If she is coming, my advice to you is to leave the children who are so well known, here, and if you want to strengthen the company simply add Ruth Fielding to it as soon as she can be spared. You could bring her up yourself. To add to my troubles, Mr. Hipwell is coming Saturday, and the children will be four times as hard to manage after he arrives. I never began to get things running straight but somebody had to come "butting in" and bothering me.

I have swapped dates this week between the Sinclair & the Highland House, to please the former, so that the Sinclair people have Wednesday night, Aug 19 & the Highland has Friday, Aug. 21, instead of vice-versa. Our second matinee at the Maplewood Casino takes place tomorrow, and you mustn't expect us to equal the first one, because we never do. Let me know right away what you want me to do about the Waumbek, the Twin Mountain, etc.

There is also the "Forest Hill House" at Franconia within easy driving distance which seems to be a good "big house" and the "Look Off" at Sugar Hill, which might be worth trying. I have filled Thurs. the 27th (the night left vacant by changing the Alpine date) with the Howard. I think you had better come up as soon as you conveniently can, and go over the situation with me.

The old woman must be stopped for saying up here that her children are Dorothea Dix Children. I shan't speak to her, & I have forbidden any of the children doing so. Every hotel keeper, but one, is exceedingly nice to us all. Mrs. Hipwell is doing very well.

Yours sincerely,
Alice L. Glover

For the next week, Mrs. Glover kept Mr. Reddy informed, sharing comments made about Miss Whipple and her (thwarted) schemes.

The audience at the Sinclair was fine tonight, and we took $22.38, more than we did the first night there and more than any time last year. Mrs. Harrington wants another date if we stay after the 29th. She says Miss Whipple wrote to her and wanted to come to the Sinclair next Monday night, but she sent word she couldn't give her a date before the last of the week, and said she could come then if she wanted to.

Mrs. Harrington said Whipple told her that her children are all amateurs, but that they are the children of actors in New York, so I told her who they really are, and you should have heard her laugh. Whipple can't hurt us a mite now, we are solid at the Sinclair.

A lady at the Sinclair spoke of how pretty they all looked tonight, particularly their hair, which was all curled, a marked contrast to Whipple's "Dutch cap."

I been trimming the old woman in fair everywhere, and with good effect as far as I can judge. (She arrives today).

A guest from the Uplands came over and asked me when we were coming there again, as I told her the whole situation with regard to Whipple, & she was indignant. She said it was the Dorothea Dix Children the guest wanted, not Miss Whipple & she should get them all to tell the manager so. I don't know yet if anything will come of it.

The manager here wrote me a very nice letter, thanking me for getting permission to change the date and saying that he had put us ahead of the Portland Juvenile Concert which is coming there on Sept. 7, and that he would not give Miss W. a date until after the 10th. I am going to shut her off on the New Mt. Washington, entirely, if possible.

I am glad the Nanepashemet is "onto" the old woman's "curves".

By late August, the image of Miss Whipple and her troupe had been thoroughly disgraced, according to Mrs. Glover.

Old Nella arrived yesterday, and people say they never saw such a homely, dirty, and ill-cared for set of brats up here. She began at once on the same old lie about the children being from New York & when some people at the hotel asked me about it last night, I told them she was not telling the truth. I have told every hotel keeper about her so far, and they all favor our children except the Uplands & I don't care about them.

As August ended, Mrs. Glover informed Mr. Reddy of the stiff competition they were up against as well as her latest effort to negate Miss Whipple's false statements, like her usual phony association with the Dorothea Dix Hall.

Aug 30, 1908

Dear Mr. Reddy,

Yours from Spring Lake received, and I am delighted to hear of the success there. The only thing I am sorry for is that you couldn't get a low rate and stay there longer. Did you try West Windsor Cottage? They used to give us a rate of $1 per day.

We have been up against a pretty tough proposition this week. Old Whipple arrived Tuesday, there are two women entertainers, a man lecturer, and a colored quartet in town, all trying for engagements & getting them, there were two church entertainments, a benefit for the baseball team, a big ball at the Casino for the benefit of the Littleton Hospital, and a baseball game every afternoon, with a big windup Sat. afternoon in the form of a triple game for the championship. As the Ball ground is next to the Casino, the Saturday games spoiled our Casino Matinee.

We have managed to keep abreast of expenses but that is about all. However, we need to stay until the 5th for Old Whipple is lying right and left about us, but she is getting turned down in lots of the hotels where we have played and the others only take her out of curiosity to see what she can do and then tell us how bad her show is, and what coarse looking children she has. At Turners where she has gone for years, and where she hires all her teams, they turned her down flatly, telling her she couldn't come there until after the Dorothea Dix Children have left town, and they told me that maybe they will not have her then. A young Jew woman staying at the Highland House, who is a friend of Whipples' made a lot of trouble for us there, repeating what Whipple told her, so that we didn't have half the audience we should last night. I told the proprietor, and she was very indignant. I had to make a speech there last night because this woman told that we do not run a home any more, that we are only trying to make money to put children on the stage, that we are overworking the children and abusing them, and a lot more, which I will tell you when I see you.

There are only a few people however who take any stock in her (Whipple) and they are gradually being disillusioned. She is however, making people think she is still with us, and is even putting red braids on some of the uniforms, to make them look like ours, so for the remainder of our engagement I am making a short, dignified speech to the effect that we are the only D.D. Concert Company in the mountain, that we still run a home, much better than we ever had, that the money we earn in the summer is devoted to sending the home children into the country, and that our children in the company are not overworked, that they are happy, well-fed, well cared for, and are all volunteers, that there is nothing compulsory about it.

Much as I hate speechmaking, I am convinced by this summer that it is necessary in most places, as not half the people take the trouble to read the programs, as is unveiled by the questions they ask me. We ought to come up here the two last weeks in August and the two first weeks in Sept. or else have 2 programs, as people like to see something different the second time, if you go twice to a house in August you get the same audience, whereas if you go once in August and once in Sept. you get two different audiences. The people at Sunset Hill wouldn't come into the second entertainment when they found it was practically the same. They said "Why we saw that last week". You see, the 2 engagements were only ten days apart, which is too close, considering that we have never given but one show a season over there before. The receipts I haven't given you are Mt Washington Aug 24, $9.27 Aug 25, Hillside Inn mat $5.75 Arlington eve. $8.13 Aug 26 Bethlehem House mat $6.30 Sunset Hill eve, $7.74 Aug 27, Strawberry Hill 6.00 Aug 28, Uplands $8.88 Aug 20 Maplewood Casino mat $3.72 Highland, eve $5.38. You see we have got about all there is in the mountain for us, about 3 weeks is all we ought to stay, but under the circumstances we need to be on the ground, because the best argument we have against Old Whipple's false assertions is the appearance of our children and the work they are doing. Strangers are constantly stopping me in the street to comment on the nice appearance of the children, and the old habitués tell me there is no comparison whatever between our company and hers, either in looks or work.

By the way, she is using a lot of costumes she "swiped" from us when she left. One of the things which turned people against her up here was the fact that she was telling all over town last summer that she was going to leave us but that we hadn't found it out. They considered that underhanded. I send you one of her programs, for your consideration, with my own comments on the margin. Our engagements to next Sat. are as follows-Aug 31 Altamonte – Sept 1 mat. Columbus-eve not yet filled but will be. Sept 1 mat. Alpine, eve Turners. Sept 3 mat. Sinclair in Parkview. Sept 4 Mt Pleasant. I have a *chance to go to Twin Mt. House Tues evening and I think best, but want to talk to the manager over the telephone Monday morn before deciding. We must take at least $15 there to make good. No hotel in town has refused us anything and the only one where the management has been at all mean was the Uplands, and their attitude was very much better on our second engagement.*

We will come home Sat. on the 12.55, reaching Boston at 8.30 p.m. if the train is on time. I am the only one in the party who is homesick. The children would stay another month if business warranted, but we have got about all there is for us, and we haven't left much for Whipple.

Your friends at the Bethlehem House left yesterday & wanted to be remembered to you, Mr. & Mrs. Lehienfeld. The weather is lovely up here.

The Children all send love.

Yours sincerely,
A.L. Glover

P.S. I have taken all the matinees we could possibly get.

Mrs. Glover responded to a letter from Mrs. Sharp and recounted the culmination of Miss Whipple's undoing.

Sept 2, 1908

Dear Mother Sharp,

Yours received containing posters and am much obliged. Am tickled to death to hear that the old woman is "finished" in Spring Lake. I am trimming her up here, and several hotels have refused to let her in until we are through. I have at last succeeded getting the Waumbek, and we go there tonight. She can't get it, because it takes pull which she hasn't got. I have finished her at Crawfords', and the Mt. Washington; she will get the Mt. Pleasant, but not until so late it won't do her much good. I have sent Mr. Reddy one of her programs, which he will show you, and she is not doing "Glow-worm" up here. People up here tell me that there is no comparison between her show and ours. I have a lot to tell you: I sent Dorothy to one of her shows, & can tell you all about numbers, costumes, and everything. She is lying to "beat the cars" and I don't hesitate to tell people so.

I hope you will have good luck and a good time at Lenox etc.

Yours as ever,
A.L.G.

Another summer tour was completed. The children were reluctant to return home, while the women looked forward to it.

PART FOUR

...Boston...
Children's Concert Company
Season of 1909-10

FROM

Mrs. Sharp's School
FOR STAGE CHILDREN

748 COLUMBUS AVENUE, BOSTON

FORMERLY THE DOROTHEA DIX HOUSE

The Company consists of the following well-known professional stage children:

Juliette Day, Ruth Francis, Vera I. Morrison, Doris Horslin, Ruth Fielding, Catherine McGregor, Stella Craig, Helena Hipwell, Grace Roberts, Vera Barry, Blanche Winters, Florence Maguire, Alison Black, Edna Schultz, Mazie Lorman, Edith Blevins, Eva Francis, Louise Daly, Helen McCoubrey, Catherine Glasco, Betsy MacMurray, Mabel Robbins, Margaret McDonough, Charlie Black, Mabel Benelisha, Rena Dwyer, Vera Dwyer, Doris Lake, Elizabeth Boyle, Helen O'Neill, Lillian Burton, Lawrence Robbins, Florence Doherty, and Bessie Poole.

GENERAL MANAGER
MRS. ANNIE V. SHARP

DRAMATIC INSTRUCTOR
MISS ADA M. CAHILL, 41 Inman Street, Cambridge, Mass.

DANCING INSTRUCTOR
MRS. LILLA VILES WYMAN

ACCOMPANISTS
Miss Alice Sullivan
Miss Lucie M. Gardner

13 | CHANGES

The association faced difficult decisions, due in part to the ongoing struggles with labor laws. The amendment had stalled, and the passage of the bill appeared out of reach. This was coupled with financial woes, so the board considered a different approach, one that included discontinuing the tours.

The girls had another idea. Mr. Reddy issued a statement that a solution had been reached in answer to the tours.

> *For 17 years, the children of the Dorothea Dix House of Boston had given a series of summer concerts in the principal hotels of New England, Atlantic City and Spring Lake, New Jersey. At the start of the 1909-10 season the Association decided to discontinue them.*
>
> *The main purpose of which was to provide a summer outing for the children and to earn some revenue for the operation of the home. The children did not want to be deprived of these opportunities hence the formation of the own organization known as the "Boston's Children's Theatre Company" for the purpose of continuing the concerts and conducting a children's theatre in Boston. All the children of the Dorothea Dix house have joined the new organization and continue their concerts which has made the house famous. The entire Dramatic and Concert Committee of the house, together with the Dramatic and Dancing instructors has joined the new organization. The main purpose of the new company is to educate stage children and children of actors. During the Season of 1909-10, the new group began the ground work on a series of classic dramas of educational value, beginning with Shakespeare's Mid-Summer Night's Dream.*

The local papers announced the formation of the club, and *Good Housekeeping Magazine* featured an article about it. Arrangements were made for the 1909 summer concerts, as in years past, but with one major change: Mrs. Glover resigned from her position to pursue her own ambitions and established her own dramatics club, the "Boston Juvenile Players." Miss Gardner filled in as assistant and pianist.

Just as her predecessor did, Miss Gardner sent Mr. Reddy reports on the revenue, expenses, and behavior of the children. She was pleased with the behavior of her girls, but Mrs. Sharp, while in Portsmouth, New Hampshire, relayed a different message.

July 28, 1909

My dearest "Daddy,"

Collection $41.28. We are here at the above and the ride to Rye Beach is 40 minutes. We can make splendid connections. The cars leave at 5 minutes of 10 and 10:15 so you can get either.

The guests were very very much pleased tonight. They all thought the program was better than last year. Your friend Josh Holder was there and put 25 cents in the hat. What do you think of that?

They say the hotels at the Isles of Shoals are not half full. How does that look for you dear? We will come out all right, anyway.

The fare to Rye is 15 cents so you see it is a saving. I did not buy the girls anything. They bought a peach each with their own money. I am not going to buy them anymore and then perhaps they will begin to see and appreciate your kindness.

I wish you were here dear, honestly I do. I hated to have you go away feeling as you did, but you would not listen to me. Everything I do is what I think is right and I try to do only what I think you would like to have me do. Please do not be cross dear, but come and see the girls Friday, if not before. They all felt badly today. They did not think you were going.

We have our same rooms here and only you are lacking to make us all happy. The girls each had a bath today and stayed in their nightgowns until 5. The heat is intense, so I thought you would want me to keep them quiet. Come down soon, please do. The girls want you and you know I do, always.

With love from the girls and many good wishes.

Believe me,
"Mother"

Her disappointment continued, indicating that the children felt bad for whatever they said or did to upset Mr. Reddy.

July 29, 1909

My dearest "Daddy,"

Your letter and new programs just arrived. Thank you very much. I am so sorry about the Whitney affair, as you say, it probably means more trouble. Blake or Clark or some of that crowd.

Did you get your permit from Hull etc.? I only wish I could do all these things for you and take all the care and trouble myself. I would gladly do so if it would save you.

We leave here in an hour for the Shoals. I hope I can do very well for you there. I am so disappointed to think you will not be there Friday, that I don't care much what happens. Sorry you feel that way with the children. They feel very badly. I told them what you said in your note.

Of course you would not come if I wanted you. Perhaps you will if you knew that Miss Sullivan wants you. Oh Daddy, please don't be nasty to me dear. I cannot do anything when you are.

With love from the girls and many good wishes—always.

Sincerely,
"Mother"

P.S. Will you look up Bar Harbor dear and see if it is not an all-night trip in which case see if we cannot take the boat at Portland and same state rooms etc. I may be wrong but you will hear it all right. Will you do this for me dear please, as I cannot find out up here. Thanks in advance. The hotel bill this year $20.50 against last year, so I saved that much for you dear and I am not spending one cent.

The girls have not been out, only as I told you and they paid for all themselves. They have not looked at anyone since we have been here.

Oh Daddy, if you knew how badly I feel, I know you would come Friday. When will I see you dear to find out what you want me to do?

Miss Gardner and the girls made the trip to Spring Lake, New Jersey, only to be met with confusion from the hotel staff. Miss Whipple was one step ahead—she had attached the name of Dorothea Dix to her children and dressed them in outfits that mirrored the original attire. The uncertainty left the guests to question: who are the real Dorothea Dix children? The hotel staff soon realized that hers were not associated with the real Dorothea Dix girls.

Despite the confusion, Miss Gardner and the girls pressed on. The summer appearances concluded with concerts in Spring Lake and the White Mountains, Maine.

14 | FUTURE PLANS

At the fall board meeting, suggestions were offered for the future direction of the association. Mr. Reddy was part of the committee.

To the Board of directors of the Dorothea Dix Hall Association:

Your committee appointed to suggest future plans for the conduct of the Association has met, and carefully considered the whole subject, and begs leave to report as follows:

First: The committee found that in view of the desire of a large number of members and friends of the Association to carry on the "home" part of the work of the house. They believed it advisable to discontinue the dramatic part, and recommended that the work of the Association be strictly to provide a home for stage children and children of actors, and abandon all its connection and association with dramatic or theatrical work of all kinds.

Second: The committee further recommended that the Association be re-organized in a manner to best carry out this part of its work, and suggested that for this purpose a committee of three or five members be appointed by the President to consider the best means of carrying out the recommendation.

Third: In view of the present condition of the finances, the Committee recommends the Manager and all others be instructed to incur no bills against the Association after December 1, 1909, and that they endeavor to wind up the affairs of the Association as of that date in order to enable the Association to begin its work on some new plan in accordance with the recommendation made above.

Fourth: The committee also recommended that the present location be abandoned on December 1, 1909 and that a committee is appointed to seek new quarters and that for the present the work is carried on in a small way.

Fifth: If recommendation 4 was not feasible, than the committee recommended that the Association continue in name, and hold its meetings with the idea in mind of continuing the work at some future time.

Sixth: The committee recommended that some plan be adopted for paying up all the debts of the Association and that a deed of the house 748 Columbus Avenue be made to the present mortgagees or to someone whom they select for the consideration of one dollar.

Seventh: The committee recommended the sale of all the property of the Association not actually needed for carrying on the work in accordance with these recommendations.

The Hall went through considerable restructuring. The "Boston Children's Concert Company" had replaced the dramatics club, and "Mrs. Sharp's School for Stage Children" appeared on programs instead of the "Dorothea Dix Hall Association." These changes were the beginning of the gradual decline for the renowned Hall, thus far marking two decades of service to hundreds of stage children.

15 | DREAM

Over the years, Mr. Reddy expressed his desire to give a play that consisted entirely of children, employing the best available talent in its production. Work began on this project in the fall of 1909.

Shakespeare's *A Midsummer Night's Dream* was touted as the first production of this caliber. It included the original Dorothea Dix children under the new name of the Boston Children's Theatre Company.[3] The play featured one hundred children total and fifty players from the Boston Symphony Orchestra, directed by Gustav Strube.

This performance was considered the official farewell, given in appreciation for the support from the organization's loyal admirers. It was a grand finale that highlighted the accomplishments and talents of the children. Mr. Reddy sent out notices about the highly anticipated play's progress. The following is a portion of his remarks:

Those who have witnessed the rehearsals of The Children's Theatre Company for the upcoming Mid-Summer Night's Dream have been surprised by the wonderful intelligence displayed by these young children in the reading of Shakespeare's lines. This is particularly true of the six clowns, Bottom, Quince, Starveling, Snug, Snout and Flute. These children, whose ages range from six to eleven years never could bring out the humor of these characters without a proper understanding of the lines, and anyone who doubts whether they understand them or not should have been present the other day when this writer overheard these six kiddies having a very excited discussion as to what Shakespeare meant by some of the lines. There was a difference of opinion at the onset of course, but little Ruth Fielding, ten years of age, who plays the part of Bottom, finally won

---

3. Notables include: Alison Black, Doris Horslin, Catherine MacGregor, Ruth Fielding, Eva Francis, Blanche Winters, Margaret McDonough, Vera Morrison, Juliette Day, Mazie Lowman, and Helena Hipwell.

out after giving good reasons, and her interpretation was finally accepted with some reluctance by the others.

Little Miss Juliette Day plays the part of Puck. Doris Horslin, who became famous in the character of "Little Lord Fauntleroy" has one of the leading "boy" parts as Lysander. Then there is Vera Barry, Helena Hipwell, Alison Black, Margret McDonough and others. There are twenty-three children altogether in the principal characters, besides a large number of children in the dances, which are under the direction of Mrs. Lilla Viles Wyman. The chorus numbers are under the direction of Mr. Gustav Strube, the well-known conductor.

Mr. Lindsay Morrison, who is rehearsing the children, is probably more interested in this performance than in all the big productions with which he has been connected. Mr. Morrison is responsible for the splendid production of this play at the Empire Theatre several years ago and is determined that this one shall excel even that most excellent performance. None of Shakespeare's plays is well adapted to children as the Mid-Summers Night's dream, and particularly when performed with the incidental music by Mendelsohn, and more especially when that music is played by fifty of the musicians from the Boston Symphony Orchestra. Probably in no other city in the country would it be possible to get professional children enough to play the parts. Boston is fortunate in having its Children's Theatre with so many of these children that it will not be necessary to call on amateur talent to fill any of the roles.

It may not be generally known that Mr. Ben Greet, the famous English actor, is a great admirer of the professional children who come from Boston. The children of The Boston Children's Theatre, who were formerly known as The Dorothea Dix Children, have particularly excited his admiration for their splendid dramatic talents. He has frequently sent for them to go to New York to fill important roles, and has often expressed that he preferred these children to any he has seen anywhere else.

The news of the performance travelled throughout Boston. Patrons were seeking tickets before they were printed. Of course, news about the newly formed theater group had piqued the interest of many patrons, friends, and writers. Mr. Fredrick J. Haley, a magazine correspondent, wrote to Mr. Reddy about writing an article on the girls.

Dear Mr. Reddy:

Referring to our conversation by telephone this morning. Will it be convenient for me to call on you sometime Monday or Tuesday and gather what information I can about the Children's Theatre? I believe this article can be made very interesting and if I am not too late to secure photographs before the children leave for abroad I shall attempt it.

Thanking you for your courtesy.

Sincerely,
F.J. Haley

Theatergoers showed concern about securing seats for the play. Inquiries, such as the one in this letter, asked about availability.

January 4, 1910

My dear Mr. Reddy:

If there are any seats left over for your children's performance of "Mid-Summer Night's Dream" would it be possible for you to give me some for my Settlement Class of girls at the Hale House? They are reading the play with the intentions of acting it and I am very anxious that they should see your performance, if possible.

I have heard and seen so much of your performance already that I am looking forward to seeing the whole of it with great pleasure. It is all so beautiful.

Sincerely,
Virginia Tanner

While the play was in production, Mr. Reddy made plans for six girls to participate in an educational tour and released an announcement.

The Dorothea Dix Children's Educational Cruise

Arrangements have just been completed whereby six of the Dorothea Dix Concert Children of the Boston Children's Theatre will join the White Star line sixth Winter Cruise to Spain, the Mediterranean, Egypt and the Holy Land giving their famous concerts in all the principal hotels en route including: Funchal in Madeira, Cadiz and Servile in

Spain, Gibraltar, Algiers in Africa, Valetta in Malta, Athens in Greece, Constantinople in Turkey, Smyrna, Beyrout [Beirut], Haifa, Jaffa, Jerusalem, Alexandria and Cairo in Egypt, Palermo, Naples, Rome, Ville France, Nice and Monte Carlo.

The company will sail from New York, January 20, 1910 on the White Star Line Steamship "Arabic".

In addition to the concerts given ashore the children will give at least five concerts on board during the cruise and will also perform in all the principal cities of Europe returning to Boston about May 1st 1910. The children will keep up their school studies while abroad and will have the advantage of all the educational benefits to be derived from a visit to some of the most interesting countries in the world.

16 | THE PLAY

A Midsummer Night's Dream was proclaimed a remarkable success. The performance was given before 2000 people at Boston's Symphony Hall on January 8, 1910, at 2:30 p.m. The sold-out performance included some of Boston's elite society: Mrs. Larz Anderson, Mrs. Jack Gardner, Mrs. H.E. Converse, Mrs. Bryce Allen, Mrs. Charles F. Aldrich, Mrs. Wirt Dexter, Mrs. Charles A. Kidder, and scores of other notable citizens.

The press notices were teeming with praise for this amazing undertaking, and those in attendance gave glowing reviews.

*****

A spectacle of rare beauty and delight...Nothing could have been more ideal or better illustrated by the poetic beauty of the play than the fairy scenes...The spirit of the play was charmingly portrayed...they gave evidence of their splendid training. Nothing could have been more amusing than the burlesque death scene of Pyramus and Thisbe. Bottom the weaver made a great hit.

*****

Gauze dresses and silver wings that sparkle under the lights made the little children look like very elves and each entrance on the stage and each musical number was roundly applauded by the big audience.

*****

It is the first time "A Midsummer Night's Dream" was ever given entirely by children. So spirited and finished was the performance that the audience unconsciously accorded them the highest of praise. That is to say, the spectator forgot they were children. Applause was generously bestowed and richly deserved by every member of the cast. Ruth Fielding, as Bottom, was a delicious buffoon. She acted the part with skill little short of genius. Although only a small girl, not for an instant did she forget the strut of self-importance and the downright unyielding faith in himself that marks the weaver. The audience was in a perpetual giggle all the time Bottom was on the stage, save when the giggle rose to a roar. Her performance was artistic to a degree amazing in so young a child. She never over acted but she "made her points" with the unerring precision of a veteran player.

*****

One of the most interesting and amusing entertainments imaginable. All were letter perfect in their lines and the intelligence with which they spoke them as well as the lack of self-consciousness in their acting were a constant surprise.

*****

It is true that other performances of this play particularly in the Hull House, Chicago and the Children's Theatre in New York have been given by children, but some of the most important parts have been filled by adults. This is particularly true of Bottom, a very difficult part for a child to play. But this production is fortunate in having a child-actress who can play the part and do it well. She is already famous as a child-actress…Those who miss this performance miss the treat of a lifetime.

*****

All in all the experience was unique. The huge hall well filled; the imposing Symphony players; the witchery of the Mendelssohn overture; the large, singularly flat looking stage always open to the audience-then a flare of the footlights, a hush like an indrawn breath, and a performance of Shakespeare's play was given that is probably without a duplicate. With a kind of critical curiosity we began to listen. We were determined to lend our most respectful attention; our utmost toleration; our most illusion-giving imagination, to help the little actors out. Before the scene was done, however, we found ourselves in a strange position. The child actors would have none of our kindness. They scorned it. They came as any other actors, and asked of us the same judgments and our sympathies, not because they were children, they compelled because they were actors. Before we knew it, they had transferred our attention from themselves as objects of curiosity, to the play. And as the well-known wrongs of Lysander and Hermia, Demetrius and Helena, poured forth, we were in the swing of the good old story, entirely at our ease because they were, without tremor, or hesitation.

    By the time the second scene was on, they were doing something their elders do not always do; they were amusing us vastly and finding for themselves genuine entertainment in our amusement. Can anyone forget the utter ease and sangfroid with which Bottom, age eight, Peter Quince, but little more, and their bully band of gnomes actually gave us genuinely comic and humorous characterization. With the fairies we were treated to still another kind of pleasure. No longer men and women and bully gnomes, here our little actors showed themselves indeed the very children they were, with all childhood's grace and charm, and for the most part the unconsciousness of it. Tatiana and Oberon flit upon the stage, a whole train of shimmering fairy forms in their wake. Puck, the blithesome lilt and alluring voice gamboled in dance and poetry with equal felicity. The tiniest of Moths and Mustard Seed upon record answered in the tiniest of voices to fairy question. And when the whole party fell asleep, draped in rose-garlands and be strewn with scattering flower petals, Bottom with his ass's ears in their midst, and Oberon says to Puck: "See'st thou thus sweet sight?" The irony of it fell quite away, and the audience rippled in sheer delight. The fairies slept about their glittering mistress, save one small baby peering innocently at the audience.

Mr. Reddy's dream had come true.

17 | AFTERMATH

Not long after the highly successful play and before the cruise, theater managers, along with the public, realized the effect the law imposed on the entertainment profession. Reporters competed to be the first to get the story.

January 7, 1910

My dear Mr. Reddy,

Will you please tell me when you can see me regarding the article in this week's Transcript (Tuesday or Wednesday) on "No More Stage Children" and tell me how it will affect the Dorothea Dix Association and the steps you intend to take, if any? It seems to me that here is a very good chance for a good story and if you will assist me I shall appreciate it greatly. I have never forgotten your kindness of a year ago, and this is a time when I need all the stories I can get, for I have been working regularly for the Boston Sunday Globe since Oct 1st.

Mr. Town has been sold out of the position he had held for 12 years and the outlook has not been very encouraging. I know it is not necessary to enlist your sympathies in order to have you respond, but I thought if you realized how vital it is that I should get all the stories possible that you would make it possible for me to get the desired material. Will you do it please?

Sincerely,
Lillian Leslie

P.S. I have evidence that the Transcript article may hasten other reporters to you on same subject. Will you not talk or write me as soon as possible. One dislikes to have others get ahead of us. L.L.

By February of 1910, the *Boston American,* the *Boston Herald,* the *Boston Post,* and other leading newspapers carried articles about the effect the law would have on children. An article in the *Boston American,* excerpted here, expressed the viewpoint shared by many on the education of stage children:

> People need to examine and look at what opportunities are being deprived. One must look at two sets of children: factory workers and stage children. A young boy working on a breaker, picking out coal and filing his lungs with dust, wearing out his vitality, using up his strength and childhood has been deprived of opportunity. It is reasoned that a little girl, put to work in a mill and placed in front of a machine that ran at high speed, endangers her delicate body and undeveloped nervous system at risk, in order to keep up with the machine. The chances of wrecking her life and childhood are real. Her health and spirit are deprived of opportunity in the future. This is what many children have to bear. To allow children to do certain kinds of work means to deprive them of opportunity later, and to deprive society of healthy men and women.
>
> The other aspect of deprivation is a child deprived of opportunity when forbidden to work. This applies to children employed on the stage or in other public performances. Looking back at famous musicians and actors, their craft was developed in childhood. Success is a combination of inheritance and childhood experience.
>
> Beethoven, Mozart and others of the world's great geniuses were prodigies in childhood. They worked hard as children, and it was necessary that they should work hard, necessary even that they should give public performances in their childhood. To have forbidden that would have been to deprive them of opportunity.
>
> If a father or mother kept a child working at manual labor four, five, six, or eight hours a day, that would be a crime against the child, and the parent should be punished.
>
> Yet the same child might be compelled by the same parents to devote six or even more hours a day to work at the piano or the violin, and that work would mean the child's opportunity for success later.
>
> Naturally, a child, regardless of all financial conditions, regardless of all considerations whatever, should be protected in its health. But a hard and fast rule forbidding children to

appear in public under reasonable restrictions is as foolish and absurd as the ordinary child labor system is brutal.

The trouble is that the agencies and the agents that undertake the protection of children are often too much given to self-advertising and to the seeking of notoriety.

Societies for the prevention of cruelty to children will make a tremendous fuss over some child legitimately earning a living, without harm to itself, on the stage, and make very little fuss over the fate of tens of thousands of children exploited and ground down by remorseless money-making scoundrels.

A child well cared for, well fed, properly educated, appearing for a few minutes or hours in some public representation that does not tax its strength or exhaust its vitality, enjoy full opportunity of their development in a public career. And is getting the education that it needs.

If the societies that seek to prevent cruelty to children would devote the money, energy and determination to the brutal child labor that destroys the child's body and brain, they might well pay less tearful attention to children engaged in public performances that develop the brain and do not harm the body.[4]

In a *Boston Herald* article published on February 20, 1910, John Craig, who succeeded Lorin Deland as manager and leading man at the Castle Square Theatre, provided these sarcastic remarks: "By all means, don't let any more children come on the stage and take those who are on it off and put them to work in some nice factory. Don't let them begin work till 6 in the morning and keep them at it till 7 at night. They'll enjoy it so much better than walking around a horrid stage for two minutes and their health will improve wonderfully. They will notice the difference too, when they get $6 a week instead of $12, $25, or $50."[5]

More supportive statements came from Francis Wilson and Ellen Terry, both respected actors who approved of children on the stage.

Francis Wilson: "I am as much in favor of the protection of children, as any father of a family could be, and for that reason respectfully submit that a law that protects one child and injuries another is not a good law and should be repealed or modified.

---

4. "Children on the Stage – Foolish Legislation Deprives Them of Opportunity," *Boston American*, February 19, 1910, GenealogyBank.

5 . "Actors Believe in Stage Children," *Boston Herald*, February 19, 1910, GenealogyBank.

The decision of the Massachusetts Supreme Court by which a few moments of daily artistic endeavors by children of the stage with the drudgery of the child in the sweatshop, the factory and the mills. There the child was indeed a beast of burden. This has led the national child labor committee into misstatements of facts that ought not to go unchallenged."[6]

Ellen Terry: "I should like to see these people in ashes who say that it is wrong for children to appear on the stage. Children who are on the stage a very well taken care of and if they were not acting, they would probably be following their natural inclination and dancing on the street. Children require close guarding any place, and their development depends entirely upon the parents. There is nothing about the atmosphere of the stage itself that demands more careful guardianship that in any other atmosphere that surrounds them during their tender years."[7]

---

6. "Actors Ask Opportunity for Genius of the Child," *Boston Herald*, February 21, 1910, 3. GenealogyBank.

7. "Defends Stage Children – A Suffragist, but Not a Militant One," *Boston Herald*, October 27, 1910, GenealogyBank.

18 | THE TRIP

By the time the news about the fate of stage children and the home was written, the farewell cruise was underway. Back in Boston, the citizens were grappling with disbelief that this organization would soon cease to be.

Mr. Reddy, Mrs. Sharp, Annie Sullivan, and the six girls embarked on their worldwide adventure from New York on January 20, 1910, on the White Star Line Steamship the *Arabic*. The *Arabic* was the sister ship to the *Titanic*.

The girls' schedule was filled with performances on the ship as well as in the countries they visited. In Cairo, they were invited to entertain at a charity ball hosted by England's representative to Egypt, gaining the highest praise from the elders in the dramatic profession.

Mr. Reddy received a note from Grace Croucher, one of the girls, dated February 19, 1910.

Dear Daddy,

I received your postal card on the 14th of February and took it for a Valentine. I was awfully glad to hear from you. I thought you had forgotten to write to me. There has been some clippings in the papers of children going on the stage. I will send you one or some, as many as I can find. I am going to hear a lecture given by Francis Wilson at the Hollis Theatre Sunday night on "Children on the Stage."

I tell you there's a hot time in Boston. They are even giving out cards with a little talk about children and finally asks you to put down whether you think children should go on the stage and the people sign "yes" or "no." I haven't seen any of the cards yet but I am in hopes to tomorrow night (Sunday.) When I go I'll take note of all that is said and will write and tell you what was said.

Well Daddy, I have learned most of my part. I wrote to you before and told you I knew all. Well, I will know it all by the time you get this letter. I hope Doris will know something of her part for her part is longer than mine. She has 585 and I have 518 or something like that.

It's an awful hard part to learn, it has so many catchy sayings and I can't seem to get them. Goodness, it's twice as hard as "Helena."

I did have a little trouble with my ear but it's all right now. It ached and ran last Thursday night, but I guess it must have come from my cold.

Well Daddy don't forget to write to me and tell me if you are going to put on "Romeo and Juliet" because I should feel awful if you didn't send my love to you and the balance to the girls.

My best regards to "Mother" and this ends Grace's letter xxx

Lucie Gardner's letter arrived while the group was in Naples, Italy. Her note was full of school news. She assured Mr. Reddy that everything was pleasant at the home, closing with:

Give my love to Mrs. Sharp and the girls. It seems so long since you went away and we shall all be glad to have the party home again. It is an event when a postcard comes and we all share them. With best wishes for continued good health and enjoyment I am,

Yours sincerely,
Lucie M. Gardner

19 | CURTAINS

Six months after the play, Miss Whipple's efforts at her own enterprise came to an abrupt halt. That summer, her health declined and on August 10, she passed away from complications of pneumonia. The newspapers remembered her as one of the founders of the Dorothea Dix Hall Association.

After her long tenure with the Hall, Mrs. Sharp spent many years working in the Boston school system, serving on various school boards. She never remarried, and her curious relationship with Mr. Reddy cooled down. After the Hall closed in 1912, their correspondence was reduced to a few cards and letters per year.

Late in the 1920s, Mrs. Sharp opened a Tea Room in downtown Boston. She sold her business in 1929, the year of the stock market crash. On New Year's Eve, 1931, she wrote to her dear friend of her business difficulties. Her heartfelt letter articulated the admiration she felt for him.

Dec. 31, 1931

My dear "Dad"—

Thanks a lot for your very nice note of yesterday. It certainly seemed pleasant to hear from you once again.

I have never seen anything like the present conditions, I do hope this year will be a brighter one.

When I closed the Tea Room, I did not earn a dollar and the man left town and never paid a nickel for the merchandise, so it was a tremendous loss all around, just unlucky taking it at the wrong time, but it is all in the past and if things will only turn upward I can soon repay those who have been kind to me, at present I have nothing.

As you know, I have lost some very good friends, it makes one feel lost.

F.S. Snyder, a good friend of mine, is now President of the Chamber of Commerce and is trying to do what he can for everyone.

> *I went to the N.E. Trust Co yesterday and told them I should like to change the account to you, and Mr. Wright said he would get in touch with you and if you wanted to draw it I could send you a check for the account.*
>
> *Just think, if we had put that in a Savings Bond in 25 years, the time it has been standing, it would be considerable.*
>
> *Glad your slippers came in well. I will always send them to you Dad, no matter where.*
>
> *That is right, go abroad and get away from this Hell on earth which is here, enjoy yourself and forget the troubles.*
>
> *I hope the coming years will be your best ones Dad. You are so kind and good to everybody, your bread will certainly come back over the waters for all the joy you have given others.*
>
> *Good luck and God bless you Dad, for all years to come—*
>
> *Always sincerely,*
> *Annie V. Sharp*

Within a few short years, Mrs. Sharp passed away.

Mrs. Glover held various positions with acting organizations, continuing her work with the Boston Juvenile Players and conducting the Dramatics Club of Roxbury School Center. She passed away in 1959 at the age of 91.

Mr. Reddy remained involved with the girls and closely followed their careers. He continued working in his law practice on Court Street and received daily visits from the older and newer girls long after the school had closed. The girls loved to chat about old times with their "Daddy." This interview appeared in the *Boston Herald* on Sunday, December 15, 1912:

> "Daddy" are you reading the war news?" Thomas F. Reddy, prominent Boston lawyer and regarded generally as a confirmed bachelor, gravely admitted a certain amount of interest is the news from the Balkans. "Well Daddy, do you remember when we were in Con-stan-ti-no-ple and how we saw the German officers drilling the Turkish soldiers? Why, I thought they were going to make the finest soldiers and now see what's happening." And the speaker, Ruth Fielding, now about 13 years old, young enough to pronounce the name of the Turkish capital with a little pause between the syllables, and old enough to have a stage reputation behind her, went on to remind "Daddy" of the things they had seen together in Malta and Smyrna and Athens and to gossip with him about the situation at the seat of the war.

She was the youngest of the Dorothea Dix Girls who made the cruise aboard the Arabic through the Mediterranean and now that the Hall is closed she comes to the Court Street Law office every few days to talk over with her friend, Mr. Reddy, who was vice-president of the Dorothea Dix Hall when the school was in its prime, the tales the papers are telling about the places she saw in the Near East. When she finishes at school she will make the stage her profession. Another of the little group of the girls who made that trip is Doris Horslin. Boston people have been wondering what has become of her. They remember her very well as a star in "Little Lord Fauntleroy." She has played child's parts with every stock company in Boston in the last 10 years. Mr. Reddy provided a wealth of information about her and the other actresses that the public knew and missed now that the famous home and school for stage children was closed.

TALK OVER EUROPEAN TRIP

"Yes," said Mr. Reddy, Doris comes in here often and chats with me about what we saw on that trip and tells me about her work. When the weather turns cold she would say that she wishes she were in Madera or in Egypt. She also followed the war news. When we were in Jerusalem we met people who had seen her play at Spring Lake, New Jersey, one summer. She conducts a dance school in Cambridge and had charge of 2 dance classes at the School of the Spoken Word in Boston.

Of Juliette Day, "Daddy" chatted in an entertaining fashion. "She is now 18 years old and she is the leading woman with the "Yellow Jacket" company now playing in New York. She has not been in Boston since she appeared here last winter as Miss Modesty in the 'Every Woman' Company."

ALL HAVE DONE WELL

The other members of the little company who made the winter voyage were Vera Morrison, Florence McGuire, and Vera Barry. All of them have done well. Vera Morrison, who was probably as well-known as any other concert child, is continuing her dramatic studies under private instructions here in the city, and conducting a dancing school in Arlington. Vera Barry is one of the Dorothea Dix Children who now are members of the ballet of the Boston Opera company.

Few companies of girls ever had a better time than had the six who spent several months aboard the Arabic a couple of winters ago. The girls amused the guest on board with 4 or 5 concerts. They danced in Seville; they appeared in the Ghezireh Palace before many notables in Egypt. They appeared in Cairo and Constantinople. They also had the honor of an audience with Pope Pius X. They returned to America by way of Cork, Liverpool then back to London and finally from Liverpool to home. Oh, how these girls remember that experience. In the Court Street Law office they talk it over with their friend "Daddy." Daddy made the voyage with them with Miss Alice Sullivan the pianist, and their chaperone Mrs. Annie Sharp.

Mr. Reddy remarked about an unsolicited letter from the manager of the cruise department to him saying among other complimentary things: "I feel it both a duty and a pleasure to place on record the universal feeling of esteem and regard for the Dorothea Dix Concert children. Their excellent program, the un-assumed modesty and their remarkably good conduct, under the restraint of like on shipboard, which must have been more or less tedious for a child, was subject of constant remark by the passengers and a source of great satisfaction to me."

Mr. Reddy agrees, not only of these children, but also of the large number of children that came to the home. Mr. Reddy wishes it might be well known that the occupants of the home and the others who came to the home's school for instruction were destined anyhow for the stage. At the time of the operation of the law was applied to the institution, an institution by the way, which was justly famous all over the United States and which was unique, there being none other like it in the world at that time. There were nearly a score of real stage children living in the house. When the house had to close most of them went on the road with their parents. The others were placed in other schools. "I have been keeping track of these girls now that they are scattered so widely, and doubtless many in and about Boston and all over New England will be interested to know where they are and what they are doing." "Not a day passes, scarcely, but that I have a letter from one or more of them. They call me "Daddy" because of the interest I took in them. I had them summer after summer in greater or lesser numbers out at my country place in New Salem."

BOYS WERE IN A MINORITY

The number of girls kept growing and the boys seemed to be frightened away. Among the few boys that did attain some measure of distinction and in whom we feel a certain proprietary interest are Oscar Johnson, Charlie Black and Theodore Edwards.

It is the ambition of all little actresses to play "little Eva" in Uncle Tom's Cabin. The house supplied two excellent "little Eva's": Eva Frances and Grace McGuiness. Helena Hipwell is on the Keith Circuit. Stella Craig is now with a musical comedy company. Catherine McGregor is just as small now as she was when she was at the house, although now she is 18 and completing her education.

It is also pleasant to remember that Miss Whipple had under her care at one time at the Hall, Anita Thomas, who's happy boast it was, "I have played with Bernhardt."

Perhaps the greatest achievement of the Dorothea Dix Children, unless the Arabic cruise and the Ben Greet connection are excluded, was the production of "A Midsummer Night's Dream." It was their last public appearance.

Among the best friends of these stage children is the Rev. William van Allen of the Church of the Advent. He appeared on their behalf before the legislation and before various committees. But the receipts of the support of the school came mostly from the children's concerts and they were clearly professionals and therefore the Child Labor Laws was enforced especially against them.

The children were guarded carefully. They went nowhere without a proper chaperone. Their house was a real home and they loved it with a tenacity of affection in many cases superior to that of a child to which a home comes as a matter of course.

Miss Whipple resigned from the work of the house a while before its suspension and went to New York to start a similar enterprise. But she scarcely began her work there when she died.

Mr. Reddy fondly remembers Mary Miles Mentor and the correspondence he had from her. He recalls the many great actresses that began life on the stage as mere children, Maude

Adams for one, Annie Russell and Ellen Terry. No one can tell just what may come of the stage children who can remember so affectionately the Dorothea Dix House here in Boston. Boston remembers them and is confident by expectations of their success will not be disappointed.[8]

A much later article, also from the *Boston Herald*, centers on life after the school and the dedication of the new theater at Mr. Reddy's home in New Salem:

> Tucked away in the wilds of New Salem, Massachusetts, far from [the] busy stream of traffic and yet only 80 miles from Boston, there has just quietly come into being an exquisite little theater that sports a distinction few others for children can boast, namely and existence that doesn't depend upon box office receipts, or upon subscriptions.
>
> Nestling on a wooded hilltop in an unspoiled New England Village that has just one store, no railroad through its center and not even a trolley or bus line and in which the honk of an automobile horn is only occasionally heard, this sturdily fashioned playhouse is nevertheless destined to be the workshop of future stars of the American stage.
>
> Even as the ink employed in this story is drying, we have seen dainty and talented little misses-children of the stage, if you please, dedicate their playhouse with two private exhibitions of highly developed stage art that at once take rank with the best Broadway has to offer. And until the Boston Herald tells about it, Broadway will not even have heard of this remarkable and distinctive theatre.
>
> Deeply appreciative, these little actresses dedicated the treasure house to their beloved "Daddy", whose generous pocketbook has provided it for them. "Daddy" sat in the front row intently watching the artistic spectacle before him. Now and then he modestly applauded, but that was all. He may or may not have realized that here before our eyes, while a horse-drawn buggy of ancient vintage or an automobile occasionally drew up to the solitary village store across the quiet street, had come the big climax in a long career devoted to the welfare of hundreds of stage children.

---

8. "Dorothea Dix Girls go on though Hall is Closed," *Boston Herald*, December 15, 1912, GenealogyBank.

Once he leaned toward us and whispered, "This is my fun." These four little words, its truth represents the one and only dividend that "Daddy" receives for the money he spends, but to him it is a big dividend for it is his greatest enjoyment. It is his contribution to the good things in life. Bright eager children of the stage whose minds and bodies are clean; children who dance, children who sing, children talented in dramatic work or comedy; children in short, who expect to make the stage their life work—these are the lucky humans "Daddy" has built a theatre for.

And now the time has come to introduce the "Daddy" of the little playhouse on New Salem hill, where "Broadway and forty-second Street" meets, minus the crowds, the box offices and the advance press notices. None other than Thomas F. Reddy, Boston lawyer and world traveler, who would much rather have his name omitted from this story, couldn't be done without spoiling it.

"The children are supreme here," he told us as he at first balked at having his picture taken.

"Please daddy," chorused Audrey June Hackett of Arlington and Ronayne Corbett of Somerville, dainty 7-year-old misses who helped dedicate the new theatre. "Daddy" finally gave in.

We sat amazed as we watched two performances dedicating the little theatre on New Salem hill. The artists, and they are artists in the true sense of the word, happened to range in age from seven to 14. Grace, strength, charming poses and gestures, freedom and naturalness in every movement, difficult acrobatic work made to look easy, and bewitching costumes featured in numbers which included toe and dancing, interpretative dances, ballets, dramatic recitals and singing.

Audrey June Hackett and Ronayne Corbett, each 7, was the youngest in the group. The others were Ruth Anderson, Malden, 11: Jeanne Maguire, Medford 11: Betty James, Somerville 13: Vivian Glassman, Cambridge 13: Barbara Allen, Somerville 12: Eleanor Largess, Medford 14: and Catherine Ward 14, Medford. Between now and Labor Day several more groups of youthful performers just as talented as those who happened to be present at the dedication, will arrive in New Salem.

It must not be assumed that "Daddy" Reddy, as he is known and always called by all acquainted with him, has just begun helping stage children. He has been deeply interested for years, but because of his modesty, much too little has become known publicly about his benefactions. The great climax of his activities, however, his theatre for children, is now disclosed for the first time.

Under direction of Mr. Reddy, the Boston Children's Theatre Company was organized 23 years ago. The cleverest of the youngster from the former Dorothea Dix School for stage children and children of actors became members of the company. They made a tour of foreign lands, performed before royalty, and were highly successful. Though Boston-born the organization centers its activities at Mr. Reddy's beautiful home in New Salem, the children passing their summer vacation there at his expense, meanwhile developing their stage work, and now, to crown it all they have a marvelously beautiful theatre of their own, which should Mr. Reddy care to fill it, will seat an audience of 200.

Many of the 400 or more children who have been guests in New Salem have become celebrities, the most celebrated perhaps, being Mary Miles Minter. Inez Courtney "movie" star is another and there are many many more. Happily, several of the early members of the Boston Children's Theatre Company are still with it, and were present at one or both of the dedicatory performances of the new play house.

Mrs. Doris M. Horslin Hackett of Arlington, mother of Audrey June Hackett, made the foreign tour with the company, and now works [as the] dramatic instructor of the present children.

Mrs. Hackett, who was Miss Doris M. Horslin when she was a stage child herself, Miss Corbett, who in private life is Mrs. Mary V. Burns and Miss Sullivan, are all highly successful women in their individual professional work, but they are never too busy to go back to New Salem to help "Daddy" Reddy and his children of the stage.

Mr. Reddy is a bachelor. He is a native of Boston, but years ago bought a substantially built farmhouse in New Salem as his home and has been adding to it ever since, until now he has what is really a private hotel of 30 rooms filled with treasures from all parts of the world he has bought during his travels.

Chief among these is an oriental room filled to overflowing. Oriental rugs cover the floor. Wall hangers have been brought from Egypt, Morocco, Turkey and other foreign lands. Eight brass lamps from Egypt hang from the ceiling. Beautiful paintings by foreign artists, tall vases, tapestries, candlesticks, bric-a-brac and floor cushions are arranged with striking oriental effect.

Even copies of intensely interesting works of art found in King Tut's tomb have places in this oriental room in the wilds of New Salem, Massachusetts. There now repose in Mr. Reddy's collection two beautiful miniatures inlaid chests exactly like chests taken from Tut's tomb, except for size. They were made in Egypt and bought there.

Combined with the theatre, Mr. Reddy has a library of no less than 6000 volumes including one of the finest collections of books on the theatre in the world. There are many volumes in it that go back to the earliest of theatrical history, books long since out of print which cannot be replaced, and rare books that are priceless. On the walls all over the building are prints of early actors, as well as hundreds upon hundreds of framed pictures of stage children who have been guests in New Salem. And all this is to say nothing of many bound volumes containing some 7000 photographs of them.

Mr. Reddy lives at his home in New Salem, 1200 feet above sea level, between June 1 and Labor Day each year entertaining children of the stage selected by his assistants. There is of course a waiting list. The remainder of the year he lives at a Boston hotel while attending to his law practice. He travels extensively, in many part[s] of the world.

In addition to his home in New Salem, he owns 150 acres of land which include playgrounds for his guests. When he returns to Boston in September he places his property in charge of caretakers who carefully guard it at all times. August 17 next will be a particularly merry day at the play house on New Salem hill, for then will be held the annual reunion of stage children there, with the beloved "Daddy" Reddy hurrying from one point to another making sure that all his little guests are happy.

One may wish to know just what kind of children these youngsters are in the company of others, away from their serious minded work on the stage. How do they act at table in their "Daddy's" big dining room, where as many as 25 may be seated at one time? How do they act at play? Are they bold or aloof? Are they "fresh" or silly? Do they put on airs and think they're smart?

"Well, if you would like to see children at their best, here they are. Good manners are just as important to them as their dances, poses, songs, or dramatic work on the stage. They know when to speak and when to keep quiet, which is a whole lot more than many highly educated adults know. They are discreet in what they say and how they say it. They are jolly, but never silly. Slang? They don't use it. Suggestive? Never, either on the stage, or off. Appreciative? Indeed they are."

"Daddy" Reddy never knows as he strolls through the long corridors of his big home, when some happy little miss may come pattering around a corner and plant a resounding smack on one of his cheeks. It is all perfectly natural just the way it should be. Model child-like in all its fine aspects is one of the biggest of the big things in the big Reddy home in the wilds of New Salem in Franklin County.

And so ends the story of a modest big hearted man who is doing much good "where Broadway meets Forty-Second Street," in New Salem, minus the box office, crowds, and advance press notices.

And having viewed this amazing spectacle from every angle, we who write about it wish that more of the world could be patterned after it.[9]

---

9. H.R. Surles, "Where Child Actors Reign," *Boston Herald*, July 30, 1933, 42, GenealogyBank.

PHOTO ALBUM

This section contains 32 photos related to the Dorothea Dix Hall organization and its members.[10]

The last home of the association, 748 Columbus Avenue, Boston, MA.

---

10. Photos are taken from (1) the author's personal collection; (2) Turner, "Dorothea Dix," 699-702; (3) Lilian Leslie Tower, "The Lonely Children of the Stage," *Good Housekeeping Magazine*, July 1908, 666-670; (4) Conrad Reno and Leonard A. Jones, *Memoirs of the Judiciary and the Bar* (Boston: The Century Memorial Publishing Co., 1900), 125; (5) "The Church of the Advent – Rectors of the Parish," Church of the Advent, accessed August 23, 2018, http://archive.theadventboston.org/histdocs/rectors.htm

158 | *Unwrapping the Past*

The school room at the home.

Part of the girls' dormitory.

Reverend van Allen, President of the Dorothea Dix Hall Association.

Thomas Frazier Reddy.

An early photo of the girls in 1905.

The girls usually traveled in groups of eight—six girls and two chaperones.

Left: Little Mazie Lorman was known for her clever impersonations.
Right: Doris Horslin as Little Lord Fauntleroy, a role that made her a favorite among theater fans.

Left: Louise Worthington (a.k.a. "Little Winkie").
Right: Ruth Francis as Editha in *Editha's Burglar*.

166 | *Unwrapping the Past*

Left to right: Ruth Francis, Catherine McGregor, Baszion Fleece, and Doris Horslin.

The Dorothea Dix girls at the height of their popularity in 1908.

Ruth Fielding and Florence McGuire as Bottom and Quince.

Margret McDonough, a lovely Dorothea Dix girl, circa 1920.

Another lovely Dorothea Dix girl, circa 1920.

Mr. Reddy's home before renovations, circa 1910.

172 | *Unwrapping the Past*

The house after renovations, circa 1920.

Mr. Reddy (left, sitting on wall) with the girls and guests.

174 | *Unwrapping the Past*

A corner of the Egyptian room.

The enclosed porch on the first floor.

176 | *Unwrapping the Past*

The dining room, where French was spoken.

Mr. Reddy and the girls playing cards at the kitchen table.

Mr. Reddy with some of the girls.

The girls in New Salem.

180 | *Unwrapping the Past*

Mrs. Sharp (center) with the girls.

Margret McDonough visiting the Stowell farm.

182 | *Unwrapping the Past*

Possibly Mrs. Glover (right) and Mrs. Hipwell with the girls.

A group of the girls playing in a New Salem field.

184 | *Unwrapping the Past*

The girls strike a pose on a little wagon in New Salem.

Another happy group of Dorothea Dix girls in New Salem.

Mr. Reddy (far back seat) with his brother, Bill, and the girls in his touring car.

EPILOGUE

On October 12, 1940, Mr. Reddy passed away at his beloved home in New Salem. His brother remained there until his death in 1949. My parents purchased the Reddy's home in 1956.

A portion of the house had been torn down for aesthetic reasons, much to my father's disappointment. When asked about the purchase, Dad boasted that he bought it "lock, stock, and barrel!" I don't think he realized the range of wonderful stories that occupied the attic space.

One year, my parents entertained the surviving Dorothea Dix girls at the summer home. I recall four or five older women reliving memories of their time spent there. What lucky girls to have had their "Daddy," Mr. Reddy, an anchor of stability in their younger years.

I found one last letter from an original Dorothea Dix girl addressed to my parents. This is the backstory: My dad, William Albert, was an Episcopal minister. The president of the Dorothea Dix Hall, Rev. William van Allen, was also an Episcopal minister. In the summer of 1958, twenty-three young girls from our church spent a four-day weekend at our summer home. That weekend revived memories of days gone by; the old house sprang to life with jubilant little girls.

At the suggestion of Alison Black Marshall, a neighbor and former Dorothea Dix girl, my mother wrote to Grace (Croucher) Mickle, another Dorothea Dix girl, about the weekend spent at the Reddy house.

Sept 12, 1958

Dear Grace and Robert,

Alison Marshall was so kind to give me your address. She thought you might be interested in the event that took place at the old Reddy home in July. My husband and I now occupy the Reddy house and use it as a summer home. My husband and I reside in Meriden Connecticut, where he is an Episcopal minister at All Saints Church.

I have always been interested in the history of the Dorothea Dix girls, and Alison has filled me in on her memories of Mr. Reddy and the school. She really thought that you would be delighted to hear about our special event held from Tuesday July 15th to Saturday July 19th. We had 23 little girls spend 4 days at the house. They are members of the Girls Friendly Society which I am the head of.

The girls slept on the upper porch in bed rolls and the house was jumping! There were games, outings to the lake, hiking, and entertainments. On a beautiful evening we had a large campfire and a weenie roast. Alison Marshall gave a little talk on what it was like to be a Dorothea Dix girl. Our girls were mesmerized by her stories of the school, stage work, and Mr. Reddy. I am sure that you have some very fond memories, I would love to hear about them.

My husband joins me in wishing you and Robert the best of health and happiness for many years to come.

Sincerely,
Rev. and Mrs. William Albert

This is the last letter from an original Dorothea Dix girl.

Sept 25, 1958
Waco, Texas

Dear Rev. and Mrs. Albert,

Your very kind letter of Sept 12th has been burning in my heart ever since it arrived!

Just imagine! Twenty-three little girls at the Reddy house for four days in July! I get a lump in my throat just thinking about it!

I was so in hopes of seeing you when we made our trip back east last summer…we made a trip to New Salem from Boston, visited for a few hours with Mrs. John Marshall…(Allison Black)…drove up the common to the old Stowell farm…the beautiful view from there of the Lake! I roamed around the Reddy House by myself…the front porch had flower arrangements as though they had been recently put there…I walked to the back of the house, wondering what our little theatre looked like now…my room, the last one down the hall closest to the barn. Everything had the appearance that the house was in occupancy, I even "felt" people…perhaps you were on a shopping trip in Orange? Alison didn't think you were there…but…the fresh flowers?

You are very kind to ask me to tell you about our memories of the House and of our School in Boston. If I ever opened up I would flood you with letters...you'd be sorry! But this little remark...I guess I was ten or eleven years old, my first trip to New Salem and one of Mr. Reddy's guests that summer was the President of our School...an Episcopalian...Rev. William Harmon van Allen, Church of the Advent, Brimmer St. Boston.

I am reminded of the dying King James the 5th of Scotland, when told about the birth of his daughter Mary, he said (speaking of the Stuart reign) Ay, it came in wi' a lass and it wi' go out with a lass! ...New Salem came into my life with an Episcopal Minister and I suppose (and hope) it will go out with an Episcopalian Minister...only I hope it is a long way off for all of us! It is so good to know that you are there...and the twenty-three little girls!

My husband joins me in wishing you and your family every good wish...and also for your happiness in the Reddy House.

"Lang may you lum reek"! ("Long may the smoke come out of your chimney!")

Sincerely,
Grace and Robert Mickle

BIBLIOGRAPHY

"Actors Ask Opportunity for Genius of the Child," *Boston Herald*, February 21, 1910, GenealogyBank.

"Actors Believe in Stage Children," *Boston Herald*, February 19, 1910, GenealogyBank.

"Children on the Stage – Foolish Legislation Deprives Them of Opportunity," *Boston American*, February 19, 1910. GenealogyBank.

Church of the Advent. "The Church of the Advent – Rectors of the Parish." Accessed August 23, 2018. http://archive.theadventboston.org/histdocs/rectors.htm.

"Defends Stage Children – A Suffragist, but Not a Militant One," *Boston Herald*, October 27, 1910, GenealogyBank.

"Dorothea Dix Girls go on though Hall is Closed," *Boston Herald*, December 15, 1912, GenealogyBank.

Reno, Conrad and Jones, Leonard A. *Memoirs of the Judiciary and the Bar*. Boston: The Century Memorial Publishing Co., 1900.

"Summer Hotels on Fire," *Daily Kennebec Journal*, August 15, 1907.

Surles, H.R. "Where Child Actors Reign," *Boston Herald*, July 30, 1933, GenealogyBank.

Tower, Lilian Leslie. "The Lonely Children of the Stage," *Good Housekeeping Magazine*, July 1908.

Turner, Margaret Storrs. "Dorothea Dix Hall in Boston," *The New England Magazine*, February 1905.